insideOut

underwear and style in the

tre
isiness, Arts &

CITY

contents

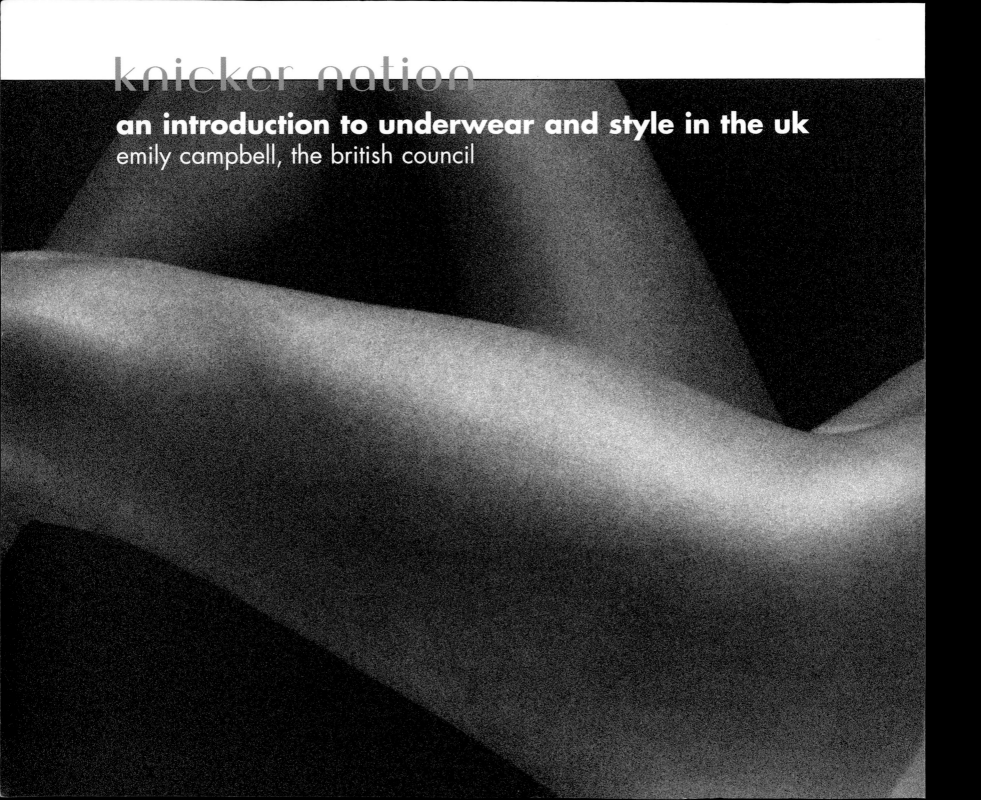

knicker nation

an introduction to underwear and style in the uk

emily campbell, the british council

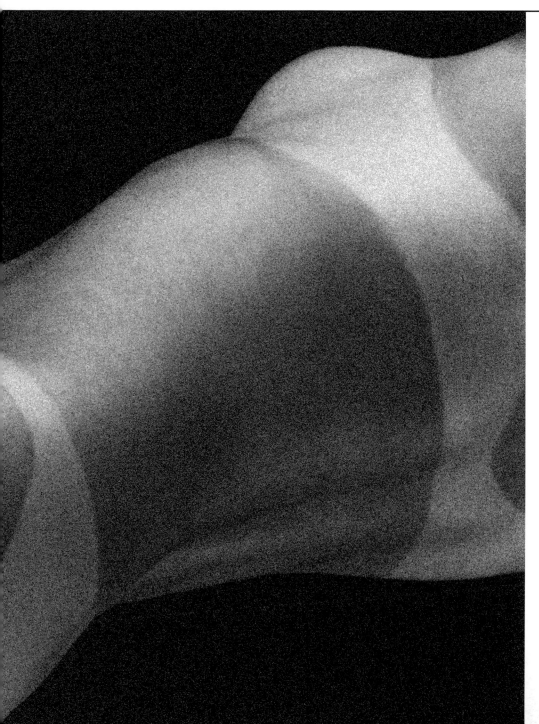

think of underwear in the UK? Marks & Spencer. Solid, abundant, nice enough but not lovely. Public schoolboys and civil servants, stiff and puerile by turns, the not-so-phlegmatic Englishman embarrassed by the erotic unless it's rude. The Englishwoman who never quite gets it right dress-wise. These days you might think of a certain kind of modish, adolescent androgyny, tough and grungy. But style?

Underwear and style in France: from the gamine cottony stripes of the supermarket to classy boutique lingerie it's clear that dressing properly is so important in France that your underwear can't let you down. There's always a mild whiff of adultery but French underwear's much more about decorum than about sex. In Italy you think La Perla, very 'lady', very luxe—olive-skinned continental models, luxuriant brunettes in lots of lace and ribbon with a strangely upholstered appearance, given they're so scantily clad. In Japan? Knickers from vending machines. The USA? The sportsbra, wholesome muscle-cladding Calvins and a pre-eminent practicality possibly more dowdy than our own.

Underwear in the UK is different. It abets not so much narcissism as exhibitionism. Not luxury and elegance but a kind of native revelry—personal, aesthetic, semiotic. Vivienne Westwood, John Galliano and even Agent Provocateur are above all glorious parodists in a great British tradition of dressing up.

Vestal, vampish, girlish, boyish, antique, futuristic, monochrome, contrast, seamless, constructed, flat, bouncy, plain or fancy— underwear gives us unlimited personae.

For all this parade of personal identity, the fact is that most (well, about 43%) of us are wearing Marks & Spencer underneath. Stephen Armstrong has described the great significance of M&S on the material culture of Britain, where it and underwear are practically synonymous. But not content to accept that M&S is merely the path of least resistance we asked some serious fashion photographers to present M&S as a serious fashion option for this book. Their propositions are compelling, though only one of them attempted the brief with, as it were, a straight face.

Stephen Bayley and James Pretlove comment with gusto on the critical relationship between the comic and the erotic in Britain. Inevitably, breasts come up a lot in this discourse. Our uplift industry is the biggest in the world, we invented the Wonderbra and its successor the Ultrabra, and if you read the tabloids you'd believe cleavage is a national obsession. Is it just that busts are getting bigger, or have our aspirations changed radically since the English poet Stevie Smith wrote in the 1930s with a different archetype in mind: "This Englishwoman is so refined/She has no bosom and no behind."?

And what, you might well ask, is the political argument of all this? Similarly non-conformist. Angela Carter thought Janet Reger's work utterly degrading. Reger thinks the eroticised woman is the strongest power-icon there is. We celebrate the lacing of Hollywood stars by Cosprop into the roles of constrained nineteenth century women. Meanwhile Westwood, McQueen, Whitaker Malem and Agent Provocateur all create corset-like erotic gear that is definitely modern armour. It's designed to make you look strong, not weak. The dominance of female gendered imagery in the book is regrettable and significant. We've really tried, but men's underwear is simply not a live design area. Someone should do something about that.

'Maverick' is the term most frequently applied to British designers and commercial artists in the international context. I find it an irritating and elusive word, but the ludic threads in literature, comedy, film, fashion and design drawn together by underwear provide a clue. This is the nation that has produced centuries of powerful erotic writers from John Donne to Jeanette Winterson, but that also offers a highly prized literary award for bad sex writing. It explains a lot about our status as a design nation—a collection of individuals who were never really comfortable with the cool propositions of modernism—that we care less about form than about ideas, fertile contrasts and a good joke.

dual controls

the place of the bosom in the british erotic landscape

stephen bayley

"No-one" as Gershon Legman said

in his classic *Rationale of the Dirty Joke*, "needs to be told that the female breast has become... the principal fetish of male attraction."

Of course they don't. We all know that here, appended to the ventral area between the bottom of the rib cage and neck, are to be found on mature women a pair of fleshy sacs that in observation, touch, feel and (perhaps mostly) imagination are the compelling landmarks of the greater art of a man's erotic landscape. In the male's endless and arduous search for sexual gratification, the breasts are beacons. This sexual role is doubly charged, semantically enriched and oedipally muddled by an unavoidable relationship to motherhood and to matters so deeply buried in the id that surgical rather than psychoanalytical techniques might be required to locate them. A fetish indeed, these breasts. They are a means of enchantment. They possess magical powers. They are reverenced beyond rationality.

All of this is magnificently resolved in that curious word 'bosom' whose suggestions of agreeable homeliness and intimacy are nicely complicated by a surreal sort of onomatopoeia. 'Bosom', with the symmetry of those double Os and the generosity of its sound, is perfectly suggestive of the warmth and weight and, indeed, symmetry of the breasts. Yet it is also revealing of the hilarious irrationality of human desire. Men may enjoy them— 'fun bags' is one current vulgarisation—but unlike the primary sexual organ, for much of the woman's life the breasts are redundant fatty tissue with little practical function. Really more of an encumbrance which has created a huge international industry of support garments.

But the bosom, as anthropologist Lionel Tiger observed, generates social as well as erotic power. This is perhaps a modern reflection of a universal primitive understanding about the benefits to survival of the tribe of having fruitful women around. This first found expression in the bare breasted mother goddess which is the subject of the oldest art we have. Later, the many-breasted Diana of Ephesus was, if you like, a multi-cylindered Ferrari to the caveman's single-cylinder Benz, expressive of the advances in civilisation. The positive associations of the breast were, of course, also later assimilated into the Christian cult of the Virgin. The bosom suggests not just the potential for erotic riches, but the existence of material wealth as well.

Poets, as it were, make great play with the ambiguities of the bosom. Robert Herrick noted "That brave vibration each way free." Algernon Swinburne wrote mesmerisingly of the "deep diversion of prodigious breasts." James Joyce's Penelope has stream-of-consciousness bosom when she "put my arm around him and yes drew him down to me so he could feel my breasts all perfume yes and his heart was going like mad." Gavin Ewart caught the bosom's delicious tension between cosiness and naughtiness when he wrote:

Miss Twye was soaping her breasts in the bath When she heard behind her a meaningful laugh And to her amazement she discovered A wicked man in the bathroom cupboard.

And Adrian Henri, in his marvelously batheic *Song of the East Lancs Road*, said "I wanted your soft verges, but you gave me the hard shoulder."

To resolve the bosom's conflicting, but complementary, tasks of performing both maternal and erotic duties on behalf of Male kind, the British have tended to incorporate certain comedic elements into the culture of the breast. While in America Marilyn Monroe had completely unambiguous sexual energy, a stunning association of innocence and availability, her nearest British equivalent Diana Dors, was more like a dinner lady done up for Hollywood, at least as Hollywood was then understood in the parlours and lounges of Maidenhead and Pinewood. It was the difference between James Dean and Billy Fury, between Elvis and Cliff. Or danger versus docility. Yes Diana Dors had an *enormous* bust, but it was a joke not an irresistible come-on.

Alas Sigmund Freud did not know Barbara Windsor, but—even more than Diana Dors—this tinseled and bleached and beehived British comedy turn represented in the amplitude of her mountainous bust the explicit British awe and the deeply repressed British anxiety about the bosom. She made you laugh, but did not make you sigh. Besides, even if the censors of the day had allowed it, an exposed nipple was not part of Barbara Windsor's repertoire. Her bosom was, symbolically speaking, blank.

Freud is the source for the belief that there is substantial oedipal complexity in organs which simultaneously signal motherhood and, when revealed outside the context of lactation, suggest sexual availability. Psychologists believe that the link between motherhood and sexual gratification (to both parties) has its source in the sense of touch common to both breast feeding and to fondling. They were keen to demonstrate this by experimenting with the physiological and neural links between the breast and the primary sexual organs. Mad German scientists attached electrodes to the nipples of volunteers and measured the consequential contraction of the uterus to prove the act of suckling produces in most women a voluptuous sexual response.

The bosom may be stuffed with only secondary sexual characteristics, but it has a primary role in both genders' preoccupations with sex and style. The basis of the attraction was understood by Blumenbach who, in his study of London prostitutes published in his *Anthropological Treatises*, declared that "precocious venery", what we would describe as 'putting it about a lot', enlarged the breasts.

To appreciate the curiosity of the British bosom, the French example offers an instructive comparison. As if to prove they are more at ease with hedonism and sex, the French have a huge literature on the subject. An early authority, was Mercier de Compiegne, author of *L'Eloge du sien des Femmes*, but the leading modern authority on mammaraological matters technical, artistic and sexual was G.J. Witowski, author of among others: *Anecdotes historiques et religeueses sur le sien et l'allaitement*, 1898; *Les seins a l'eglise*, 1907 and a synthetic English language volume called *Tetoniana–medical, literary and artistic curiosities of breasts and breast-feeding*.

We have no native studies of such depth or authority. Moreover, the cultural differences–perhaps even an inferred inferiority–between bosom and *poitrine* are reflected in the slang annexed by the bust. While the French have bizarre *ropolopots*; magnificent *nichons*; feminine *miches*;

exciting *tetons* and seductive *doudounes*, we are more likely to have tits. Again, the association is comic rather than sexual. There is a 1714 usage for tit meaning a 'pleasant fellow' and according to lexicographer Eric Partridge, its use as a blokish word for breasts can be traced back to "Australian low colloquial" usage. These same Australians have supplied us with an agreeable alternative to tit, more amiable, less abusive. Etymologists argue about its origin, but it seems likely that the wonderful word 'norks' was inspired by Norco, a brand of butter popular in New South Wales whose wrapping shows a cow with an ample udder. Australian English is even more robust than American. In her 1962 book, *The Delinquents*, Criena Rohan has a character say "Hello, honey, that sweater—one deep breath and your norks will be in my soup."

The Americans are, if anything, even more mixed up about the bosom than the British. An internal 1993 memorandum from Fox Television was picked up by the satirical *Spy* magazine. The memo concerned a forthcoming programme about women with notably large breasts and the author was concerned with the station's 'Standards and Practices' lest any lapse might affect viewers and advertisers. His pronouncement was Solomonic in wisdom. This Prince of Political Correctness said that while the words tits and knockers are *not* allowable, no exception would be taken to boobs, bazongas, jugs, hooters and snack trays.

Just as lascivious humour is the British male's defence against the British woman's powerful and disturbing combined arsenal of sex and motherhood, so it is equally revealing of something profound in the British and their observations of taboo that underwear has to be disguised in foreign language. And that language is, one is tempted to say, 'naturally', French. We have no proper English word for the *brassière*, nor for *lingerie*. And as philologists might insist, a language which has no words of its own to describe something has no natural understanding of the concepts in hand. Thus, in the same way as *liason*, *affaire*, *enceinte* and *petite amie* have entered our vocabulary of erotic discourse, so *brassière* and *lingerie* conveniently combine evasive sophistication and wince-inducing coyness.

There is a big human history of concern about underwear and about gender relations with certain types of clothes. The Bible tells us that "a man who putteth on a woman's garment becometh an abomination."

Indeed, with the image in mind of Federico Fellini (by no means a conventional heterosexual) who enjoyed making love while wearing a bra, we might agree. But underwear can be put to all manner of imaginative uses in man's battle to understand and consume the bosom. Literature's best description of the powerful erotic associations of underwear is Philip Roth's. In his 1969 tale of adolescence, *Portnoy's Complaint*, the hero uses one of his sister's bras to secure the bathroom door while he masturbates. Disturbed in his act by a knocking on the door, Herrick's consequential brace vibrations set up in the tensed bra only increased his manual frenzy.

But the reality of underwear is really rather dire. Exposed bra straps are near the top of the list of motifs which have a powerful counter-erotic character. There is not a woman, nor perhaps a fat Italian filmmaker, on the planet whose attractiveness is enhanced by the exposure of these joyless elasticated belts. They do not imply suspension of a gorgeous, firm bosom, rather the brute depressing mechanics of flesh and gravity. These prosthetics of lingerie are grim—and often grubby— bookmarks of the humdrum. Careless exposure is not titillating, but depressing evidence of incipient and unpromising slatterliness. And thus we are back to the question of an ample bosom and its relationship to precocious venery.

Perhaps only in Britain with its specially complex attitude to the bosom could the recent Wonderbra poster campaign have become a national phenomenon. Britain is still, after all, home to millions of men who stand and gawp on foreign beaches at what continental men ignore. I know I do. It was in Britain that an extremely pretty, but in fact rather skinny, Czech model was translated through an adman's fetish into a symbolic figure as resonant of the bosom as Diana of Ephesus. With hair and make-up, pouting lips and the extraordinary mechanical advantage of the Wonderbra which gives vectored thrust and powerful cantilevers to otherwise unremarkable lunchtrays, Eva Herzigova became the personification of the New British Bosom.

Sexy? Most certainly! But wasn't it simply the picture of the delightful model. It was the copyline too. The 'Hello Boys' was very revealing in the use of the masculine diminutive. This was an imprecation both enticingly erotic and, of course, utterly maternal. So, on forty-eight sheet posters up and down the land, the British males

HELLO BOYS.

THE ONE AND ONLY
Wonderbra

THE ORIGINAL PUSH-UP PLUNGE BRA. AVAILABLE IN SIZES 32-38 ABC

Leigh Bowery in a spoof
of TBWA's Wonderbra
campaign for Blow magazine,
1994

ambivalent attitude to the British woman's bosom was made explicit.

I asked one of the country's leading fashion designers, Caroline Charles, about this. She introduced a new term into the fashion debate. Like the tit it has ornithological associations. She spoke of 'pigeons'. Apparently, many models have breasts like pigeons. Although this sounds like a bad translation of Omar Khayyam, Ms. Charles meant small, pointy odd little things that were difficult to dress. Women with breasts like pigeons look as though a cocktail frock has been draped over a corner of Trafalgar Square.

Breasts like pigeons are, to the couturier, as much of a problem as breasts like saddlebags (the sort that flop inelegantly over the side of the ribcage). The great thing about the Wonderbra is that it gathers up the pigeons and scoops up the saddlebags and, to use Ms. Charles' interesting additional contribution to the similes, organises them so they point forward with the dedicated beam of 'headlights'.

So Wonderbra was not really about sex at all, but about organisation. We are, the British Bosom shows, fundamentally a practical nation.

reasonable prices for a reasonable nation

stephen armstrong

To Britons, there are certain constants, certain undeniable truths in a changing world. There is tea. There is humour. There is the desire to soak our minds in alcohol to forget who we are. And there is Marks and Spencer. Let's not mince words here. There can hardly be one living Briton who hasn't consumed the brand name St Michael. Grandmothers may stumble over the pronunciation of Nike and sweet toothed children may fail to raise a hopeful smile when offered a bite of Fry's but to a united United Kingdom, St Michael means one thing: it means pants.

Ah, St Michael's underwear. The knickers that cover 43% of British bottoms. The first great brand that most of us encounter on our voyage through consumer capitalism. St Michael's are the pants that your parents bought you and that defined your groin for the years before you cared what was under your trousers. How well school children remember the joke about the young nun who is ravaged by a rampant angel. The following morning she reports the incident to Mother Superior and says that the angel has informed her that God demands she do it again tonight. "How do you know it was an angel?" queries Mother Superior. "It was written on his underwear", the novice replies.

And St Michael is British. It could have been created in no other country. Where else would a store issue a manual to its manufacturers which dictates how much bottom coverage every pair of knickers has to have? Which other nation's manual would insist that the knickers elastic be strong enough to survive 1,000 washes? The St Michael name was created—along with the short-lived and rather too continental St Joan brand—to enhance the British way of buying. It was a step by Marks & Spencer to remove the wholesaler from the store purchasing equation in the cash poor 1920s and pass the savings on to the recession stricken customer. It became the first of the store's six principles as laid down by Simon

Marks and Israel Sieff—"to offer customers, under the brand name St Michael, a selective range of high quality, well designed and attractive merchandise at reasonable prices."

Reasonable prices. That's what we wanted. Reasonable prices for a reasonable nation. If the British prided themselves on anything for most of the last century, it was their reasonableness. Which other Imperialist power would have fudged and fumbled their way out of a mighty Empire in as bloodless a way as possible, trying to do the decent thing by all concerned? And as they were doing so, M&S was with them all the way.

During the war years, St Michael meant 'utility clothing'. In an incredible genuflection at the altar of Marks, the government's instructions on the making of the rationed, sturdy clothing that citizens could purchase with their coupons copied the standard specifications M&S had been issuing to their manufacturers. Throughout the 1950s, Marks & Spencer reached the peak of its innovative powers, bringing the new man-made fibres over from America and hurling them out into the mass market in nice, sensible undergarments at a reasonable price. St Michael was born of the pragmatism that defined a nation of shopkeepers and where else would shopkeepers shop but at Marks and Spencer?

And yet, the century wasn't one of joy unbounded all the way for St Michael. It wasn't entirely a century of consumer and reasonable pricing shopping together in perfect harmony. Because, at the end of the 1990s, the humble and pragmatic Briton became far less humble and far less pragmatic than before.

They wanted fun and sex and holidays and un-British things like stripped pine floorboards and expensive foreign lager.

They wanted the glamour of international labels, whether they saved up to buy them or nabbed them in bargain bins at Matalan out-of-town discount warehouse buying clubs dressed up as fashion stores.

And so St Michael died, killed more effectively by sex and shopping than by any vengeful demonic power from below. At the end of the Millennium, M&S gave up the lonely struggle and called in the professionals. Specifically, they called in Joseph Corré and Serena Rees who make up the steamy lingerie sensualists Agent Provocateur. Corré—son of Vivienne Westwood—and Rees rose to the occasion and came up with the Salon Rose range. It's an explosion of lacy knickers, sultry, patterned suspender belts, trouser-boiling thongs, electric-violet and fuschia-pink mesh basques, scarlet bras overlaid with black lace, glitzy bikinis, wet-look one pieces, baby-doll nighties and the sheerest of stockings. Come Valentine's Day 2000 and the Kensington M&S had sold out of its entire Salon Rose stock. Marks and Spencer's underwear department could breath again, although their breathing had become noticeably heavier.

But this is supposed to be about the things that never change, and in a sense that is what's really happened at M&S. Despite the lust that suffuses our faces when we stroke our way through the Salon Rose range, we can rest comfortably in one great, British constant. Whereas Agent Provocateur briefs cost 25 a pair, Salon Rose skimpies will set you back a mere six British pounds. An extremely reasonable price indeed.

Photographers Jeremy Murch, Hugh Hales-Tooke, Ben Ingham, Sandro Sodano and Platon were commissioned to photograph Marks & Spencer underwear for this book.

vested interest

gym class with the generic brand

photographed by jeremy murch

if the nude is rude,

why are knickers naughty?

angela carter

existence—indeed, the chronic persistence—
of the cultural taboo against nakedness that
seems universal to all people at all times.
In symbolic terms, a penis sheath or an
ochre body rub is as good as a white tie
and tails.

We may see a stark naked man who
perceives himself adequately, even
impeccably, dressed. In the same way, a
woman covered from neck to ankle in a
woollen dressing gown or housecoat
wouldn't dream of going down to the shops
for a packet of tea because she perceives
herself as dressed in a provocative manner.

Robert Graves prissily distinguishes
between two kinds of unclothing. The naked
(he poetically opines, I leadenly
paraphrase) is sacred but the nude, rude. In
other words, the pagan spectacle of the
ritually and consciously unclad is the human
in a glorious state of holy nature, which is
why it is taboo. The nude, dressed up to the
eyeballs in a lengthy art tradition, is clad in
an invisible garment composed of
generations of eyes.

Elsewhere, as in *The White Goddess*,
Graves describes how a numinous young
Celtic person solved an enigmatic request to
appear before her lover neither clothed nor
unclothed by wrapping herself up in a

fishing net. This non-garment performs none of the essential functions of clothing, neither protection from the elements, nor chaste concealment of the parts, nor sign of status. Yet it fulfilled, whilst it subverted, the conditions of the taboo against absolute nakedness. Similarly, Baudelaire made his girlfriend take off all her garments but her necklace. This made her look even more naked by contrast, while offering a talismanic protection against what Graves might call the unleashed power of the goddess (though in that case she was a black one). From here, it is but a step to the magical *déshabillée* of the Janet Reger catalogue.

Women's sexy underwear is a minor but significant growth industry of late twentieth century Britain in the twilight of capitalism. In this peculiar climate, the luxury trades prosper. Perhaps a relationship with post-imperialism may be postulated; some folks call it 'decadence'.

"This collection has received enthusiastic acclaim wherever an appreciation for excellence as part of life's enrichment is sought"declares the brief preface to Miss Reger's picture book of her wares.

The cover of the book depicts a handsome pair of legs in gold kid mules, caressed in an auto-erotic fashion by a hand whose red finger-nails are of a length that prohibits the performance of useful labour. The whole is sheathed in the unfolding drapes of a peach-coloured, lace-trimmed, full length negligee: the eye automatically follows the line of the leg upwards to a tasselled garter: the Rowena G Garter. One size only. Colours: snow, champagne, palest green, soft apricot, ebony. The garter—and there could hardly be a finer example of the luxury non-garment—is offered in the price list at the back of the mail-order catalogue for a mere £10.

Most of the colours of these fetishist adornments are those of the archetypal luxury non-food, ice-cream—with the inevitable addition of black which, for some reason, remains synonymous with naughty underwear. The Reger catalogue hints subtly at the naughtiness: the girl posing legs akimbo in Corinna C *négligé* Ebony has scarcely perceptible bags under her eyes, and two black clad models are pictured reclining on fur throws, perhaps to make some points about sophisticated carnality.

This luscious and expensive (£2) catalogue acts as a vade-mecum via the post to the enrichment of your life through the non-garment. In itself, too, it is an *objet de luxe*, an invitation to voluptuous or narcissistic fantasy, depending on the sexual

previous page Photograph
from the Janet Reger mail
order catalogue, c.1978

orientation of the browser. It also has enough of the air of the come-on brochure for an up-market knocking shop to risk causing creative confusion in those countries where brides as well as *négligés* are obtained through the post.

This is part of what can be called the "fantasy courtesan" syndrome of the sexy exec, a syndrome reflected admirably in the pages of glossy magazines.

Working women regain the femininity they have lost behind the office desk by parading about like a *grande horizontale* from early Colette in the privacy of their own flats, even if there is nobody there to see them.

The erotic point is inescapable. The models are dressed up in undress, in a kind of clothing that is more naked than nudity. Their flesh is partly concealed by exiguous garments in fabrics that mimic the texture of flesh itself–silk, satin finish man-made fibres, fine lawn–plus a sublimated hint of the texture, though (heaven forbid!) never the actuality, of pubic hair.

The models are very heavily and ostentatiously made up, as if to demonstrate this civilised voluntary exile from the natural. They, too, are *objets de luxe*, as expensive to manufacture as the fragile ambiguities which adorn them. (The Leliah N Nightdress, colours: rose, beige, black, in French lace, is really nothing more than a very sophisticated version of the Celtic young person's fishing net.)

More often than not they are also elaborately coifed, though occasionally in a style of reticent dishevelment, often with flowers in the hair, as if for some kind of bedroom *fête-*

champêtre. However informal they may be, these garments are quite obviously public dress.

I remember reading somewhere how, in the 'Fifties, model girls were often reluctant to do lingerie jobs. Swimwear was fine, but respectable girls drew the line at modelling knickers, on the grounds that they should only be photographed in clothes in which they might be seen in public in acceptable normal circumstances.

This rather quaint scruple seems to have vanished now. The ostentatious glamour of the new lingerie (of which Janet Reger is only the most widely publicised purveyor), and certain changes in social relations, have created a climate in which this kind of non-garment is socially acceptable. It is breath-takingly expensive, and high cost is in itself a great moral antiseptic. The rich are different from us. The single-minded pursuit of over-all excellence neutralises all kinds of waywardness.

Lingerie has become simply another kind of the non-garments characteristic of what you might call 'hyper-culture'. Others are some furs, evening dresses and ball gowns, real jewellery. All are, first and foremost, items of pure conspicuous consumption. Yet they also fulfil elaborate ritual functions.

They are the garb for the Good Life but in an opposite sense to that of the TV ecoserial–in the pursuit of anti-nature. This includes the opera, eating in restaurants, parties and, increasingly, sexual relations in which the gibbering old id, the Beast in Man, the manifestation of nature at its most intransigent, is scrupulously exiled. In hyper-culture, human relations are an art form.

The precious, costly fripperies on Harrods' underwear counter must do a roaring business among transvestites, whom I trust wear it in good health. For transvestites, the appearance of femininity is its essence. As I grow older, I do begin to believe this might be so. I'm just waiting, now, to aspire to the sexless grandeur of the ancients portrayed in Bernard Shaw's play *Back to Methuselah*.

Of course, the whole notion of the 'natural' is an invention of culture, anyway. It tends to recur as an undertow in hyper-culture times as some sort of corrective to the excesses of those who see life as an art form without knowing what an art form is. But to say that nature as an idea is an invention does not explain the idea away. Clothing as anti-nature–as the distinction between beings that are not–can be seen in action in any circus. It is amazing what a number of non-garments—bridles, plumes, tassels—even the liberty horses wear, to show to what degree they have repressed their natural desire to run away. The relations between the non-garments of circus horses and those of professional strippers is obvious: they are seldom wholly naked, either.

Even the hippies were reluctant to strip off completely in their pursuit of the de-mystification of the human body. They could never resist the temptation to add a string of beads or two, or daub themselves here and there with grease-paint. Perhaps the promotion of the non-garment as decent wear shows a streak of anti-culture within hyper-culture itself. This should come as no surprise to devout students of the whole messy business.

However, the real complexity of the taboo against nakedness may be seen most clearly in the catalogue of a firm like Frederick's of Hollywood—who, interestingly enough, use line-drawings rather than photographs. That is probably for reasons of cost, but it enables, all the same, a far greater degree of physical distortion. Mr. Frederick is the man who offered you panti-girdles with padded or 'uplift' buttocks, and padded brassieres that elevated the nipples while leaving them bare. Downmarket sexy underwear has a long, murky history.

In the early 'Sixties, even before permissiveness hit the West Coast, Mr. Frederick—a world away from Serena French Knicker and Hattie Brief—was advertising the Pouf (sic) Panty, which had a puff of marabou at the front like a bunny's tail put on the wrong way round. His scanty bikini briefs were "embroidered with lips at the nicest spot". He urged his mail order clients how it pays to advertise: "Wear out 'Try it! You'll like it!' panty! Chances are... he will!" The acetate (no natural fibres here) non-garment bore this slogan stitched athwart the pelvic area. A vogue for sloganising knickers (and, indeed, underpants) has been a consistent feature of the downmarket, 'raunchy' lingerie market for years. Just the slogans get ruder as time goes by.

Of all Mr. Frederick's offerings the most striking is the "all-nylon sheer lace brief pantie" that has "daring *derriere* cut-out edged in lace". He calls this steatopygous gesture "Back to Nature". You couldn't put the whole ambiguous message of women's sexy underwear—upmarket, downmarket or in my lady's chamber—any fairer than that.

Angela Carter for *Cosmopolitan* 1978

luxe lingerie

alice cicolini on janet reger today

Photograph for the Janet Reger mail order catalogue, c.1967 - 1970

dominated London's bedrooms, bonfires of bras littered London's streets, fuelling the furnace of the Women's Liberation revolution. From the aftermath emerged a designer whose work was to provoke by turns acres of hate mail and more than three decades of global admiration. Janet Reger had returned from Switzerland, with husband Peter and daughter Aliza, to a city where traditional moralities were being overturned in a tidal wave of political change.

Janet Reger is to all intents and purposes a more down-to-earth yet equally ambitious cross between Dynasty's Alexis Colby and Crystal Carrington. Her lingerie –"more for the woman I would like to be than the one I am"–is no less redolent of this Judith Krantz-inspired, feminine yet vampy 'mistress chic'. Reger's early life, told in disarmingly open fashion in her autobiography, was a desperate search for love sweetened by giddy professional successes. After graduating from Leicester College (now De Montfort University), her talent was sought throughout Europe. Even in the early days of her career she achieved the life of the women for whom she designed–prosperous and filled with travel, good food and glamorous company. Meeting Peter Reger,

on a kibbutz in Israel, seemed to add love, the finishing touch to this starry existence. Their relationship was passionate and tempestuous, with all the necessary romantic fiction ingredients of jealously, a disapproving mother-in-law and long-distance separation.

As a freelance lingerie designer, Janet Reger developed her reputation as a visionary, whose jewel-coloured satin nothings and wisps of lace had manufacturers clamouring at her door. Tired, however, of their constant desire to reduce her designs to a shadow of their former selves, Reger and her husband Peter spotted the opportunity to shift her creative vision into a higher gear. In June 1967, Janet Reger Creations Ltd. was born.

Immediately, Reger began to challenge accepted mores with advertising and marketing imagery that would be considered provocative even in twenty-first century Britain. Reger's label typified a nation in upheaval and expressed the sexual liberation of the early 60s, lived to the letter by Reger herself. Her lingerie 'explored and proclaimed the inherent sexual sensuality of feminine underwear' and newly 'liberated' women flocked to her boutique– along with their husbands.[1]

The sexual freedom of the period also generated a movement of women who were to be Reger's strongest critics. 'Glamorous, seductive and feminine' [2] to her fans, Reger was pilloried by the late British novelist Angela Carter as a purveyor of 'sophisticated carnality' for perpetuating an image of the 'fantasy courtesan'.[3] Not surprisingly, Reger has little positive to say about her detractors:

"I've never understood the now rather dated feminist attitude that to look great is un-liberated. Most of the successful women I have met certainly make an effort to look as lovely as possible."

Her daughter Aliza, who now runs the business, fully supports her:

"All these women's libbers were saying 'How can you make sexy underwear? It's derogatory to women, it's beneath their dignity, makes them into sex objects'. And Janet said 'No, it puts them where they want to be. Yes, to be sexually attractive for your man, but I'm totally for women's liberation. I stand in the workplace, I earn my own living, I don't depend on anybody and I am equal to my husband'."

It has been argued that Reger's designs, epitomising as they do a very traditional vision of femininity, perpetuate an image that detracts from rather than enhances women. Janet Reger would argue that this image is as empowering to women as it is desirable to men. The Reger brand catalogue may be a 'come-on brochure for an up-market knocking shop', but the majority of her customers were and are women, and women who thrive on their ability to step in and out of this particular femininity at will.[4]

Agent Provocateur are an obvious contemporary successor to Janet Reger in the quality lingerie market, although their style has been described as more 'Cynthia Payne' than Reger's 'Madame Pompadour'.[5] The fundamental basis of these two companies is very similar. Both were established by partners—in business and in life—and their success seems to derive in great part from the projection of an image of easy sexuality, open and exploratory. Joe Corré has attributed the commercial success of Agent Provocateur to the combined male and female perspective, a sentiment with which Reger wholly agrees and one which must surely answer the accusations of Reger's detractors.

Photograph for the Janet Reger mail order catalogue, c.1967 - 1970

It is partly because Agent Provocateur's owners are exciting and contemporary that customers want to buy the product, and with it, a bit of their lives. Was this also true of Janet Reger Creations in the early years? Aliza Reger would take a more simplistic view: "I tend not to be too analytical about why people buy certain things. People mostly buy things on impulse. 'It's pretty, I like the colour and I want it'."

Evidence suggests that she's right. In spite of the critics and the difficult years-Peter's death, the financial downfall, the loss and re-gain of her brand name in the mid-80s Reger's design style has survived with remarkable consistency over the years—exquisite textures, rich, unconventional colour and improbable delicacy. No designer has manipulated these elements with such skill or with such success in the market. Reger has good reason to believe that the battle for the image of woman has been won by just the kind of powerful, eroticised women for whom she and Agent Provocateur design.

Janet Reger remains creative head of the Reger brand and is still known as 'the queen of luxe lingerie'.[6] She has directly and subliminally influenced a generation of designers and retailers. Her products cross

Photograph for the Janet Reger mail order catalogue, c.1967 - 1970

the boundaries of social aspiration and class, from royalty to Page Three girls, in a way that few other brands have achieved. It is a triumph of design, but also of an uncomplicated sexual philosophy:

"I think that our wide-spread appeal proves that regardless of class, wealth and education, women want to attract men and men want women to be attractive. I see nothing wrong in this. It works in reverse too, and it is natural for people to feel this way. It certainly keeps the world going round."

notes

1 Colmer, Michael, *From Whalebone to See-Through*, London: Johnson & Bacon, 1979.
2 www.thebestofbritish.com
3 Carter, Angela, "If the Nude is Rude, Why are Knickers Naughty?", *Cosmopolitan*, 1978.
4 Carter, "Naughty".
5 Sherwood, James, "Dear Santa, please spend lots of money", *Independent on Sunday*, 5.12.99.
6 Sherwood, "Dear".

show us your bra

photographs by sandro sodano

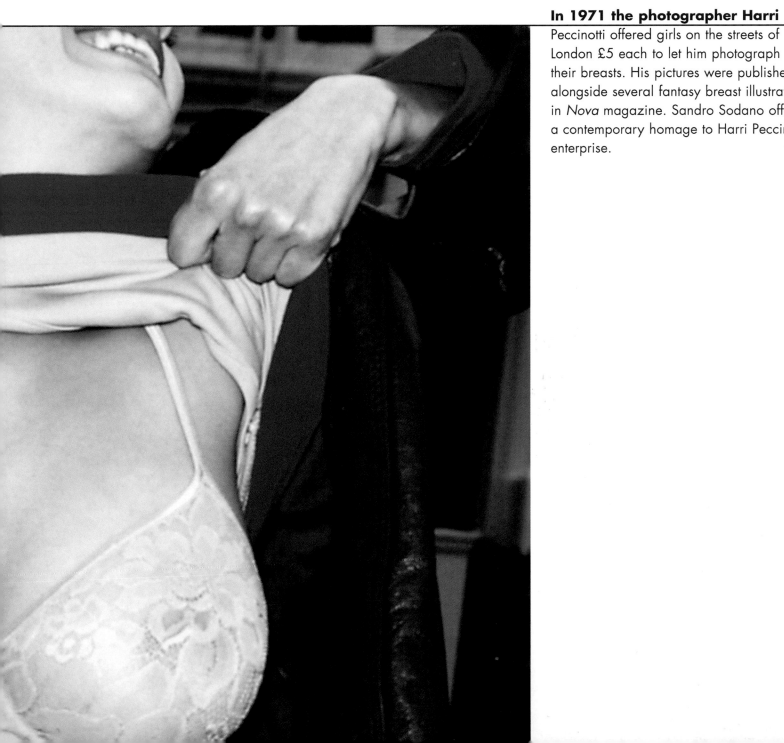

In 1971 the photographer Harri
Peccinotti offered girls on the streets of
London £5 each to let him photograph
their breasts. His pictures were published
alongside several fantasy breast illustrations
in *Nova* magazine. Sandro Sodano offers
a contemporary homage to Harri Peccinotti's
enterprise.

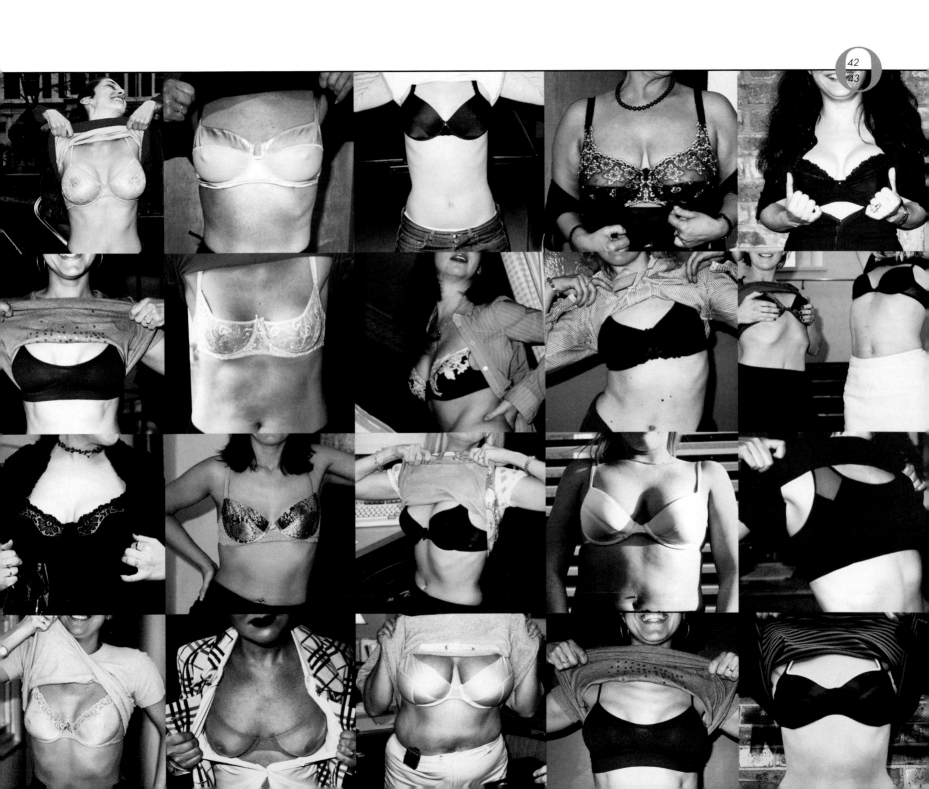

sea change

st michael on the shore

photographed by beningham

a ceremony in itself

caroline evans

*both pages John Galliano
for Christian Dior
Spring/Summer 1998*

items of underwear have mutated into
outerwear; men's shirts have been pulled
through slashed jackets, women's shifts
have turned into frills at the neckline before
evolving into blouses. Marie Antoinette's
chemise dress in Elizabeth Vigée-Lebrun's
portrait of c.1783 predates by two centuries
the baby doll dress of the 1950s and the
slip dress of the 1980s and 90s. The
transposition of underwear to outerwear
usually invokes a relation between
femininity, sexuality and display. For
although the eighteenth century royal *levée*
was "a ceremony in itself" and, therefore,
the unfastened bodice indicated informality
rather than libido,[1] nevertheless by the
1880s the artist Édouard Manet could
announce "the satin corset could be the
nude of our age."[2] In Manet's 1877
painting *Nana* the actress Henrietta Hauser
stands before her mirror, powder puff in
hand, wearing a chemise and a pale blue
satin corset while an unknown admirer in
evening dress looks on. In the late
nineteenth and early twentieth centuries
underwear became increasingly luxurious;
silk, cotton muslin or fine linen petticoats
and chemises were decorated with lace,
embroidery, shirring, ribbons and rosettes,
pin-tucking and faggotting. Underwear was

brought into the semi-public realm by French *demimondaines* as morning dresses, gowns and wrappers which were often among the most delicate and expensive items in the female wardrobe.

The history of the slip dress, and its predecessors the eighteenth century *robe volante* and the *chemise à la reine*, is the history of a garment's transition from the boudoir to the salon. In the twentieth century boudoir dress became eveningwear. John Galliano revived and popularised the bias cut of Madeleine Vionnet, whose sensuous unlined gowns of the 1920s used many of the sewing techniques of underwear. The modern slip dress was pioneered by the American designer Geoffrey Beene in the 1980s and in the 1990s by the British designer Stella McCartney, first in her own name and then in her designs for Chloé. John Galliano also created the lingerie look in his designs for Christian Dior, most famously worn by Diana Princess of Wales in a dark blue ankle length slip dress in 1996. The move from inside to outside is always bound up with questions of class, morality and, sometimes, national identity. Stella McCartney's slip dresses were promoted by the press as the signature of the 'London girl', an insouciant Portobello

Road style that was rapidly marketed as 'Cool Britannia', harking back to the promotion of Carnaby Street in the 1960s as an index of 'swinging London'. Yet for all its contemporaneity, the 'attitude' of McCartney's London girl also evokes the flirtatiousness of the French Rococo; Fragonard's painting of 1768-69, *The Swing*, teases the spectator with the image of a lover's view up the skirts of his mistress as she kicks her legs in the air. McCartney's delicate pastels and airy pallete also recall the eighteenth century French decorative arts and painting, in her evocations of femininity as fragrant, delicately erotic, light.

Amongst contemporary designers, only Hussein Chalayan has eradicated the 'lingerie' connotations of ruffled net, taking the material but changing its meaning, by appearing to sculpt geometric forms in pale pink ruched tulle, echoing his rigid plastic dresses based on aeroplane technology. Other designers interested in structure have, instead, taken the corset as their inspiration and retained the erotic connotations of underwear. The underwear influences in recent high fashion have been either from lingerie or from corsetry. The former is loose, fluid and stresses the sensual pleasure of fabric and expensive craftsmanship; the latter is a structured, rigid, carapace, which can range from John Galliano's recreation of Edwardian hourglass figures to Hussein Chalayan's experimental structure which deconstructed the idea of the corset.

Of all late twentieth century revivals, the corset is the most ubiquitous. This *leitmotif* of late twentieth century fashion was revived in Paris in the 1980s by Jean-Paul Gaultier. Madonna, in her Blonde Ambition tour of 1990, made it notorious. In Britain Vivienne Westwood introduced the corset in 1985 and used it in almost all of her subsequent collections, including her Harris tweed collection of 1987. In the late 1980s and

left Hussein Chalayan
Spring/Summer 2000
right Antonio Berardi
Spring/Summer 1998

early 1990s her five Britain Must Go Pagan collections converted the eighteenth century corset into the modern 'bustier', often printed with details from French Rococo paintings. In the 1990s the corset became a key theme in British experimental fashion, referenced by almost every significant designer who used it to trawl both backwards and forwards in cultural history. In 1996 Galliano's debut collection for Christian Dior reinvented the Edwardian hour-glass figure, but clad it with a decorative corset of Masai beading worn over the dress, part *belle époque* nostalgia, part post-colonial fusion. Antonio Berardi's early collections featured both transparent negligees worn with stockings rolled above the knee and constraining Victorian corsets, loosely based on the stays of the 1840s-60s which covered the breasts while simultaneously exaggerating them. Berardi's 1997 corset was, however, even more nipped-in at the waist and, for all its exaggerated femininity, recalled, rather the fetishised eighteen inch waisted corsets worn by Mr. Pearl, in London, and the American advertising executive Fakir Mustafa beneath his business suits. Andrew Groves' Cocaine Nites collection, based on Ballard's novel of that name, similarly featured a model

with her hands strapped together and wearing a black leather buckled corset like the bondage and fetish wear corsets which also crossed over into mainstream fashion in the 1990s. Berardi's Spring/Summer 1999 collection, by contrast, featured airy wicker corsets and skirts that sat more comfortably on the body, even as they emphasised the model's nudity beneath. In a more experimental vein, Hussein Chalayan produced a carved and polished wooden corset for his Autumn/Winter 1999 collection, fastened, rather like a flower press, with chrome bolts at either side.

Many of Alexander McQueen's collections since he graduated in 1992 featured variations on the theme of the corset or bustier. In his Highland Rape collection (Autumn/Winter 1995), based on the Jacobite Rebellion and the Highland Clearances, he showed both a tartan corseted bodice and a metal cuirass which fused corset and armour in one. The Hunger (Spring/Summer 1996) featured a clear plastic bustier with live worms sandwiched between layers against the model's bare skin. In his Dante collection Stella Tennant modelled a mauve and black lace corset suggesting the *femme fatale* of the Decadence, while its high, constraining

lapels, like an exaggerated wing collar, forced her chin up in a pose which also suggested an orthopaedic brace or truss. For Givenchy Spring/Summer 1998 McQueen produced an urban cowgirl in a yellow python skin hat with a matching bustier worn over a shirt and tie. A similar bustier in glistening black, juxtaposed this time against the model's dazzling white flesh, appeared in McQueen's Autumn /Winter 1998 London show which culminated with the figure of Joan of Arc surrounded by a ring of flames. The following season, Aimée Mullins modelled a corset made by Whitaker Malem for McQueen. Made from moulded leather, with a high orthopaedic collar, it was worn with a white frothy lace skirt. The bodice's tan leather surface bore the faint trace of nipples and navel; a diagonal gash from armhole to neck, patterned with decorative stitching, suggested a surgical suture rather than the conventional lacing on a bodice. Medical themes were played out on a body which simultaneously suggested illness and invulnerability, giving the image a darkly double-coded edge. These bodices reappeared in Givenchy's Autumn/Winter 2000 collection in which the models were styled like androids, the vulnerability of flesh

patterning the surface of an armoured red leather bodice. Another clear plastic bodice patterned with electronic circuitry traced the body's contours, suggesting the android's electronic circuitry displaced from inside to outside.

The reversal effected by underwear as outerwear also links to deconstruction in fashion in the way it brings inside to out structurally, rather than in terms of the cultural meanings associated with underwear, class, intimacy and eroticism. Richard Martin and Harold Koda argue that "deconstruction, a model of thought current to our times, provides a metaphor for the capacity of clothing to migrate between the personal and the public spheres" in exactly the way that underwear migrates between these two spheres.[3] In the early 1990s the Austrian designer Helmut Lang created complex layers of minimal net T-shirts, a 'poor' aesthetic that transformed the transparency of filmy underwear into structural questioning. Later in the 1990s, Hussein Chalayan produced a deconstructed corset-bodice that was more like an architectural structure by Frank Gehry or Co-op Himmelblau than a cladding for a body. Deborah Milner's Autumn/Winter 1998-89 collection included a black, rigilene dress, consisting of the plastic boning used in corsets sewn onto fabric; the dress had a corset inside but displayed its innards on the outside.

Yet deconstruction has not featured largely in British design which has, rather, been characterised by a quirkier and more anachronistic turn of thought. In the early 1990s the late Leigh Bowery designed little neck corsets for Rifat Ozbek's catwalk collections. Vivienne Westwood's most innovative contribution in terms of underwear has been not her corset-bodices but her earlier designs from the 1980s. In 1982 her Buffalo collection featured 1950s-style upholstered satin bras worn over voluminous layers of clothing. Westwood said the 'Buffalo' look was inspired by the dress of Peruvian women, "big women... who live in a space of their own, waiting for the world to grow up."[4] The bra she chose was an old-fashioned 'pre-liberation' bra, the kind that feminists in the 1960s were reputed to have burnt. Westwood, instead, converted it into a highly visible fashion accessory. In 1985 she pioneered the mini-crini, a short, hooped underskirt or skirt worn with a jacket and platform shoes. The hoops were plastic rather than steel and collapsed when sat upon; Westwood claimed the skirt was eminently practical and that she bicycled to work in hers every day. The look was widely copied by contemporary designers, often in the form of the puffball skirt which retained the silhouette but lost the resonant meanings of the garment. Westwood's mini-crini was a hybrid of the hooped crinoline of the mid-nineteenth century and the 1960s' mini-skirt. It brought together competing mythologies of women's oppression and women's liberation in one garment that conflated two sets of ideas about female desirability: one about covering, the other about uncovering the female body. In later collections she experimented with ways of altering the body's silhouette, for example in her famous 'bummies', a small, collapsible cage worn on the bottom and based on the hoops and bustles of earlier centuries.

A comparable exploration of the cultural meanings of the human body emerged in the designs of BodyMap, set up by David Holah and Stevie Stewart in 1982. BodyMap clothes hugged the body but had holes in unexpected places to explore the relationship of flesh and cloth; these clothes relied heavily on Lycra wrapping the body in unexpected ways which, while not overtly referring to underwear, mimicked its

characteristics. Their designs of the mid-1980s prefigured Alexander McQueen's Spring/Summer 1998 collection which wrapped the body in cutaway Lycra. The same collection, in which models were drenched by 'golden showers' of spot-lit water, featured McQueen's signature fringing that evoked the showgirl's costume nudity rather than the boudoir intimacy of underwear, a look that he developed in fringed and appliquéd leather for Givenchy Spring/Summer 1998.

In 1976 punk girls had suborned fetish wear as part of street style, mixing mini-skirts and suspenders, fishnet and bondage straps, corsets and safety pins. Throughout the 1980s, London's Soho, home of the Raymond Revue Bar, Madam JoJo's and Saint Martins College of Art, was a prominent zone for street fashion. 'Deviant' underwear, drag and cutting edge fashion jostled each other on the same pavements; the emergent 1980s club scene shared the same commercial premises as strip joints and drag clubs. Londoner Tim Woodward launched Skin Two in 1983, initially as a club for serious fetishists; ten years later it had expanded to include a shop and an internationally successful magazine, as fetish wear moved into the mainstream market. The previously covert repertoires of S&M, bondage and fetishism became fashion, pure and simple. Without that, the high fashion incorporations of underwear into outerwear, described above, could not have happened in the 1990s. The French fashion designer Thierry Mugler even contracted with the London-based House of Harlot, founded in 1992, a fetish wear design team who specialised in rubber and the 'pump-up bra' they invented.

Fashion and fetishism have in common an interest in artifice, masquerade, role-playing, ritual and dressing up. This crossing of marginal sexual practices into mainstream fashion in the 1990s created a commercial opportunity for significant developments in retailing. In London, two underwear shops of couture standard set up in 1993 and 1994. Their prominence and success marked the way underwear had already migrated to the mainstream in fashion. Boisvert was a jewel-like shop, specialising in luxurious European lingerie. It was furnished in French boudoir style with a satin 'corset chair' and 'pantie' footstool designed by Precious McBane, who describe themselves as 'dysfunctional furniture' designers, and who now sell in Paris, New York and Seattle.[5] In 1994 Vivienne Westwood's son Joe Corré and his partner Serena Rees opened the underwear shop Agent Provocateur in London's Soho.

Also catering to the top end of the market, and in many respects not dissimilar to Janet Reger's underwear in the 1970s, Agent Provocateur promoted an ironic Frederick's of Hollywood aesthetic, part saucy seaside postcard, part sophisticated nineties sexuality. With the jewellers Erickson Beamon, Agent Provocateur also launched a range of jewellery consisting of dog collars, handcuffs, chokers and ankle and belly chains inspired by, according to Corré, "fantasy girls, Las Vegas strippers, slaves and Dominas."[6]

While a dominant strand of 1990s fashion imagery promoted a 'bad girl' aesthetic, revelling in tacky deviance, another strand played instead with a *verité* style of social realism. British *Vogue* published an eight page spread by the photographer Corinne Day. She depicted her friend Kate Moss at home in her flat, her hair uncombed and her face bare of make-up, dressed in a series of cheap and tacky undergarments from Ann Summers sex shops. Day's documentary style which rejected the artifice of most underwear shoots was theatricalised by the

previous pages Alexander McQueen Spring/Summer 1998
left and right Alexander McQueen Spring/Summer 1998

photographer Rankin when he produced a fashion spread for the magazine *Dazed & Confused* called 'Big Girl's Blouse.' Rankin played on British social snobbery by choosing blowsy, big-bosomed models whose shirts strained at the chest to reveal glimpses of cheap bras. Both Day and Rankin were reacting against sleek and glossy commercial fashion images; both chose underwear to make their point.

The designers' work I have surveyed in this essay maps a series of polarities that have traversed the landscape of contemporary fashion: fluid lingerie versus the structured corset; inside versus outside; private versus public; *amour* versus armour; nature versus culture. These categories are neither discrete nor fixed. Rather, they are dynamic and volatile, shifting, regrouping and merging in intricate formations. As an interface between the body and dress, underwear is a mobile and fluid signifier of this complex set of relations and themes. For all its proximity to the body, nothing is more cultural than underwear. Mobilised by fashion designers in the 1980s and 1990s, it engendered a range of speculations on the themes of embodiment, sexuality, deviance, femininity and class.

Notes

1 Koda, Harold and Richard Martin, *Infra-Apparel*, pp. 28 and 30.
2 Cited in Valerie Steele, "The Corset: Fashion and Eroticism", *Fashion Theory*, Volume 3 Issue 4, December 1999, p. 451.
3 Koda, *Infra-Apparel*, p. 105.
4 *Observer Colour Supplement*, 5 December 1982.
5 Rose, Cynthia, *Trade Secrets: Young British Talents Talk Business*, London: Thames & Hudson, 1999, p. 110.
6 Rose, *Secrets*, p. 106.

film foundations

karen kay on cosprop

from London's West End, through the stuccoed surround of Regent's Park, where nannies are quietly serving up sandwiches without crusts for their charges, and towards Camden's once trendy canal-side bag and beads entrepreneurs. Onward, past a handful of café bars (the kind that could be in Cricklewood or Coventry, with rustic pine tables and brushed stainless steel serving counters), and a gaggle of tourists forcing smiling faces at a camera in the rain.

Beyond the market stalls and the tattoo parlours, we come to a red-brick enclave of shoe-box housing and gleaming 24 hour petrol stations; a Legoland village where the ordinary folk of London reside. It's a soulless patch of the city, where there seems no reason to stop unless your key unlocks one of the hundreds of front doors that front the identikit properties.

But stop I will. Beyond the roadworks and the children playing ball in the street, I reach a door that's been rapped by hundreds of Hollywood hands. So many of those familiar faces—Dame Judi Dench, Emma Thompson, Gwyneth Paltrow, Cate Blanchett—have all taken this same route, finding themselves in these alien surroundings, to place themselves in the very capable hands of a certain Mr. John Bright.

Impish and charmingly humble, Bright is the man responsible for giving Helena Bonham-Carter the somewhat cumbersome mantle of 'period actress'. He once laced her into one of his waist-clinching corsets *et voila!* she was typecast for a decade.

In 35 years as a film costumier, Bright has carved a niche for himself as the Costume Corset King. Here, from an unassuming north London warehouse, he has boned and laced leading ladies into the kind of memorable hourglass silhouettes that leave us (and them) gasping for air. Most memorably, Bright collected an Oscar for his efforts with his co-designer Jenny Bevan on Merchant Ivory's beautiful drama, *A Room With A View*, and has continued to dress the casts of all the duo's productions since, including such classics as *Maurice* and *Remains of the Day*. But, if Bright had pursued his own choice of career, he might have been collecting such awards for a very different craft.

"I desperately wanted to be an actor," he recalls sitting in the dressing-up box that is his office, "but my very Victorian father wouldn't allow me to even consider such a thing, so I had to 'get a trade'. He sent me off to Walthamstow Art School in 1957 to do a four-year fashion design course. Every evening I would sit in the library leafing through historical costume books and during my holidays, I worked in the wardrobe department at the Theatre Royal, Stratford-upon-Avon, where I first met Peter O'Toole and Dorothy Tutin.

When I left there at 21, I was expected to go to the Royal College, but I still had a passion for the theatre, so I went into the repertory theatre at Hornchurch where I was able to act and design costumes, keeping my father vaguely satisfied. After a year, I managed to get a grant to attend drama school, and I really don't know to this day how I persuaded my father to allow me to go."

While studying at the E15 theatre school in East London, Bright offered his services as a costume-maker to the Chichester Festival Theatre, started by Laurence Olivier and later to become the National Theatre. But his grant fell short of the financial requirements needed to see him through his course, and Bright found himself working at Hornchurch Theatre full-time after completing just two years at drama school. Then, in 1965, he sowed the seed that became Cosprop, his hugely successful costume house.

previous page Period-style corsets made by Cosprop *right* John Bright and employees in the Cosprop studio

"With acting being so unpredictable as a source of income, I realised I needed another string to my bow. There were two fairly big costume companies, Samuels and Simonds, that went out of business around that time, so when they were bought up, I went and bought some stock from the new owners. I think my first-hand experience of acting and my fashion training enabled me to really understand the relationship between costume and camera."

Today, Bright employs forty full-time staff and occupies four buildings in Camden totalling over 35,000 square feet of floor space filled with snaking rails of chronologically categorised costume. Here, amidst the residential streets filled with people going about their daily lives and ignorant of the proceedings behind Bright's door, hip young actors are transformed from their twenty-first century selves into Edwardian ladies or Victorian street urchins, into Second World War land girls or New Look debutantes.

Bright has collected an enviable archive of reference material, curated in a back room and accessed only with his rare permission. Fragments of lace and fragile lengths of hand-painted nineteenth century silks are carefully rolled in acid-free tissue, and cause a raised heartbeat as you watch gloved hands gently unfurl them for a treasured glimpse. Floor to ceiling boxes are carefully labelled–'50 forget-me-not corsages belonging to Queen Mary' or 'Queen Alexandra's feather fan'–and stacked beyond the reach of grubby fingers.

"I was lucky enough to be approached back in 1980 by The Ladies Guild of Gentlewomen. They'd had a selection of clothes and accessories donated by Queen Mary for charitable purposes. Alice of Athslone, who is patron of The Guild, came to me and asked if I'd be interested in having them. At the time, I only had about £800 to spend and she agreed the figure. I have a few dresses which are now insured for about £6,500 each and, because they are heavily beaded, are stored in boxes to stop them tearing under their own weight. Some of the pieces were handmade by Norman Hartnell, and have a little pocket inserted at the hip, so she could store a biscuit to refresh her when she stood for long periods at formal functions."

The Cosprop archive is also brimming with pieces by those designers who have shaped the last 150 years in fashion: Poiret, Worth, Chanel, Balmain. But for Bright, despite his obvious love of embellishment and the luxurious textiles featured in period gowns, it is the costume's foundations that provide the true fascination.

"The foundation of the costume is what shapes the silhouette, and in a way, shapes the character, he explains. Before we try on any gowns, or outer garments, we have to get the basic structure of the undergarment right. Only once an actress has been fitted with the right underwear, can we start to construct the costume that the audience will see. Even if the corset or the petticoat won't be seen, it is absolutely crucial that we get it right. When she is wearing a corset, a woman has a different poise; she sits differently, and walks differently. In layers of *broderie anglaise* petticoats, she finds an instinctive femininity that doesn't come with a sports bra and a thong."

For Bright, there is a sense of passion that goes way beyond professional pride when it comes to perfecting the wardrobes of his actresses and actors. He laughs and scorns the celluloid gossip that Gwyneth Paltrow wore a Gossard Ultrabra in *Emma*.

"It's outrageous. Her boobs would have been pushed together far too much!"

It is a minute attention to detail that sees his own garments being re-worked again and again until the maestro is satisfied with the results. In *Sense and Sensibility* for example, Emma Thompson wore very solid corsets even though the final silhouette was quite soft and draped.

"When you do a period film, you have to ask yourself what makes that time different from our own. One of the key things is the formality of days gone by. You have to help actors get into character by dressing them right from the foundation, so they understand the restrictive way people moved, and the discomfort that was endured or bulky layers that women wore. It's a subconscious translation into the mood of the era for both the actor and the audience."

That subtle mood-setting comes from the not-so-subtle—and often arduous—preparation that goes into Bright's costumes. Once pieces are made, they are repeatedly washed through to give a worn-in feel—"nobody goes around wearing brand new clothing all the time." With many of the period costumes, Bright's team of seamstresses do

Corsetry boning in Cosprop's haberdashery stockroom

any stitching that may show by hand to give an authentic randomness to it.

Then, once the garments are made to his demanding specifications, Bright will help the wearer understand the behavioural nuances that go with their costume.

"Some people instantly take to the etiquette of period costume, empathising with the clothes as soon as they are on, others have to be spoon-fed. In 1981, when we were making *The Bostonians* in America with Merchant Ivory, I had to be called on to set to advise all the actors how to sit in their corsets and trained dresses. Unlike today's slovenly approach, you have to approach a chair from the side and perch sideways right on the front of the chair, with your back bolt upright because of the corset underneath. And you have to avoid sitting on the train so it doesn't crumple."

In the forthcoming film, *The Golden Bowl*, Bright has created a series of opulent Edwardian costumes (each equalling haute couture gowns in their construction and probably worth up to £7000 in man-hours alone) for Uma Thurman, Kate Beckinsale and Anjelica Huston, starting with a corset, petticoat and bum-rolls (cushions of stuffed

calico to add padding around the hips and waist) for each actress and taking photographs that are drawn over to create suitable silhouettes for a second fitting.

"Uma has a fantastic physique for Edwardian costume. She's 47 inches from waist to floor, and has a tiny waist measurement, so we could really play with the draped bustle and train shapes. She has 28 changes in the film, so we had to make corsetry that was as comfortable as possible to build her costumes around, while remaining as true to the period as possible.

If a corset is too long in the body, it really digs into the thighs while an actress is sitting, and there can be hours and hours of waiting around on set, so we have to ensure that she is going to be as comfortable as possible. None of them have the energy to keep changing back into their everyday clothes between takes, because these costumes take a long time to put on."

Bright is also responsible for the exquisite corsetry worn by Kate Winslet in *Quills*.

"The corsets she wears feature quite heavily throughout the film, and often in close-up, so we had to make them more

visually accurate than we might if the garment were purely part of the unseen structure of a costume. We experimented a lot to make it look realistic but as comfortable as possible—especially as she had to wear it in so many scenes."

Bright based the corset on an original panniered example from 1775, displayed in the Kyoto Costume Institute in Japan, using photographs as reference.

"We found an excellent slightly slubby linen sateen that had the right uneven weave we were looking for, and then used modern quarter-inch Rigilene boning folded in half lengthwise to re-create the illusion of very defined ridges of traditional whaleboning. We burned the Rigilene at the ends and moulded it into a small globule so there weren't any sharp ends to dig in to Kate's flesh or rip the fabric.

The seamstress did use a machine for the stitching, but it was set on a very narrow zig-zag so it looked less uniform than a running-stitch, to give a more hand-finished feel. We also mimicked the 1775 example by creating a horizontal band inside the corset, across the bustline under the arms, so it 'presented' the bust in the correct way."

Cosprop's collection of antique and custom-made period-style underwear

Bright's team made twelve corsets for Kate to wear during the making of the film, ensuring the director and designer were always happy with the look. He claims he is always learning and loves the process of researching a film's wardrobe.

"1911-13 is my favourite period. It has a weirdness to it; a crankiness that's very opulent but struggling to be free and expressive. Then the war broke out and that oddball extravagance never really returned. Had the First World War not happened, I think fashion might have taken a very different path. Emancipation really came to fruition in the war, with women working in their own right as auxiliary workers. After that, fashion lost all its formality and perhaps its elegance too."

Like Bright, who may have pursued his first choice of career, we should perhaps be thankful that fate dealt the hand it did.

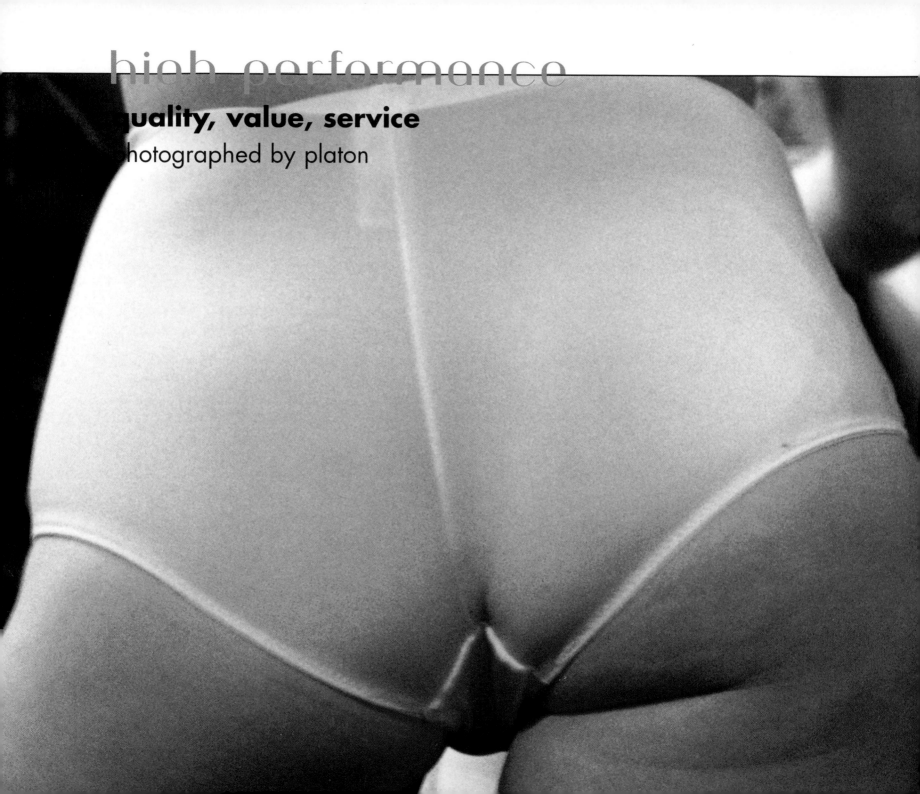

high performance

quality, value, service
photographed by platon

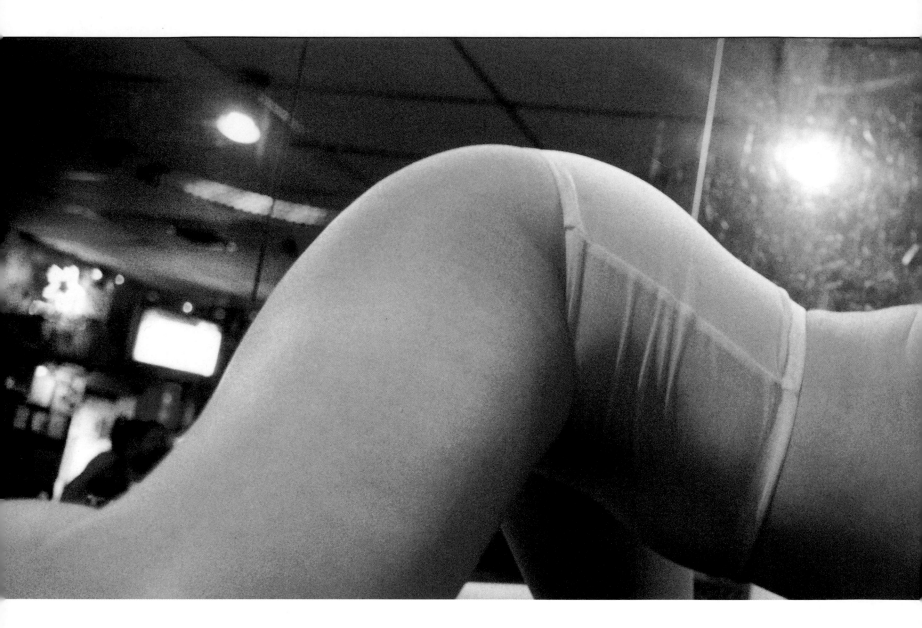

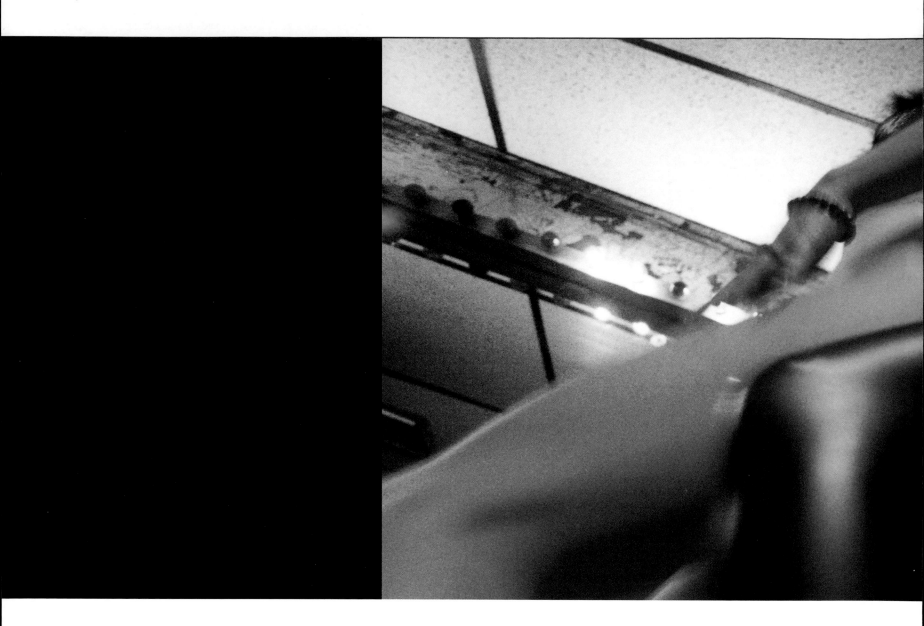

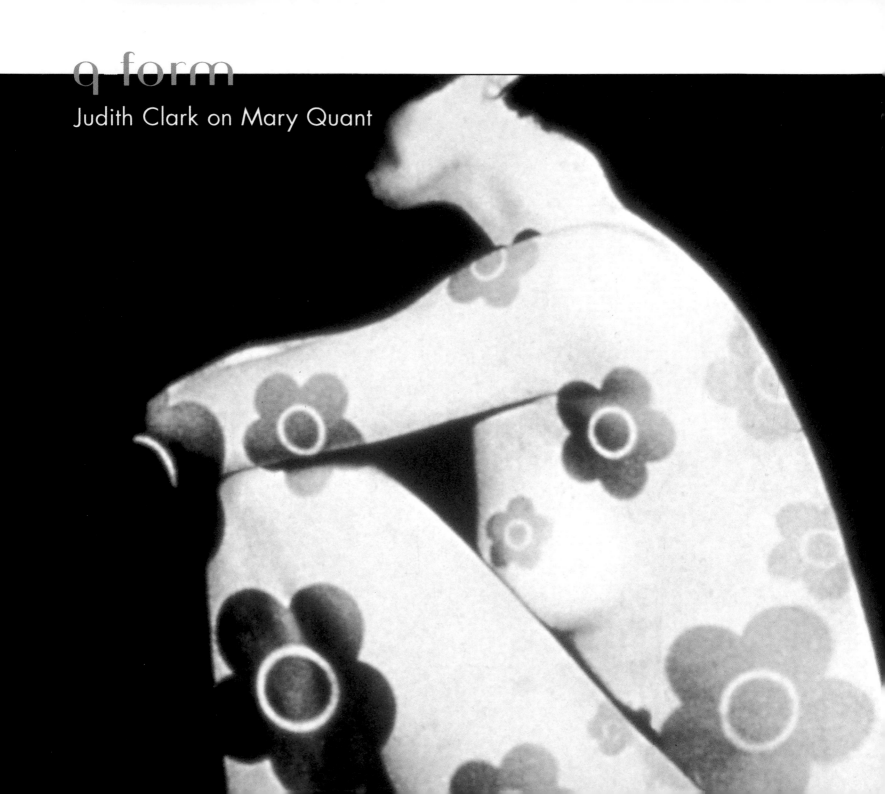

q-form

Judith Clark on Mary Quant

*'Bare essentials',
Mary Quant designs
1968*

Through sophisticated oscillation between tradition/modernity; male/female; naturalism/artificial exaggeration, rarely do clothes so eloquently reflect a *zeitgeist*. Many of the elements from her designs have come to symbolise 1960s dress. In 1963, she received the Sunday Times International Award for "... jolting England out of its conventional attitude towards clothes." On the cover of the catalogue of her 1973 retrospective exhibition at the London Museum, Kensington Palace, Quant's signature daisy was put in the place of Big Ben's face: she had become synonymous with London. I met Quant in her South Kensington studio off Draycott Avenue, now Headquarters to the Quant empire.

Art school trained, Quant set up her first boutique, *Bazaar*, on the corner of King's Road and Markham Square in 1955, with her late husband Alexander Plunket-Greene and business partner Archie McNair. Economic boom, social change and near full employment provided a young female market in search of up-to-the-minute, off-the-peg fashion. The shop was not only the locus for experimentation, but became a template for a new boutique culture. George Melly described *Bazaar* as "the only Pop manifestation in the years between Rock and the Beatles." Quant's retail success was such that it provoked 'Miss' sections within department stores throughout London.

When speaking of her work, Quant acknowledges the enormous momentum provided by the people surrounding her in that period. She was a central figure in what is described as the Chelsea Set, made up of actors from the Royal Court, rock stars and their girlfriends. When they went on tour, so did her look, creating a sensation in its wake. To adopt her style was to be a member of a club.

Mary Quant catered to a market too young for the formality of Couture and she harnessed the tension between tradition and the modernity that characterised both 'Mods' and bohemians. She played with the rules of fashion design, inverted them and radically changed their proportions: waists dropped (pioneering hipsters), and skirts rose way above the knee to create the famous Quant 'mini'. The mini was a development of the 1920s shift dress, both an expression of both freedom and androgyny. The beginning of the century from which Quant quotes saw separates and sportswear transform the wardrobes of men and women and made them more alike:

… she achieved romantic modernity by turning tradition on its head… this dualism has characterised the approach of many British designers, even the most radical make overt reference to the historical styles or traditional clothing in terms of cut, fabric or detailing.

Amy De la Haye's Introduction
to *The Cutting Edge,* Victoria
and Albert Museum, 1997

Quant nodded to the same sartorial tradition from which she was deviating: a trick that runs through a lot of British designers' work today, most extravagantly exemplified by Vivienne Westwood and Alexander McQueen. The confident motifs which decorated her styles remind us of late 1950s hard-edged abstract paintings, such as those by Elsworth Kelly, typically geometric, symmetrical and limited in palette. Her colours, however, were surprisingly subtle, resisting primary colours and looking instead to English tweeds for the development of hues such as 'Coleman's Mustard', or 'Prune'—more country walks than capsule living. Her vibrant 'Op Art' use of black and white has associated her with a sort of speculative futurism. Even her black hair was cut into graphic shapes, exemplified, of course, by the clean lines of her signature style 'five point' bob by Vidal Sassoon that she still wears today.

Quant designed a mood, evoking it through wittily and irreverently marketed products, 'Booby Traps' (bras), 'Bacon Savers' (stockings with pants attached), 'Brighton Rock' (coloured stripy knickers), 'Daddy's Girl' (pretty dress), 'City Slicker' or 'Bank of England' (pin-striped tunic). It was a total look made up of clothes, underwear, shoes, accessories and make-up.

Underwear was essential to the language of the look promoted by Quant in the 1960s, the logical consequence of a dramatically changing silhouette and feminine ideal. Emphasis was placed on a natural sporty body, rather than the constructed hour-glass figure of the 1950s. Breasts were suppressed to favour the abstract unity of the body and to enhance the modish look of youth.

New elastics—notably Lycra, which was introduced in 1959—and strong, light fabrics with stretch-and-recovery qualities allowed the development of minimal, gentle control garments. Quant embraced new man-made fibres, material that both kept its shape, and could be washed easily and quick to drip-dry.

During the 1960s, symbolic weight was placed on the bra as a vestigial corset. The association of real nakedness with naturalism and freedom (both sexual and political) provoked both the 'No-Bra Bra'—the invisible bra, as well as Quant's cleverly marketed 'Starkers' natural foundation make-up.

"Each component dictated to all others.... Underwear was of vital importance for an overall look... we wanted it to be softer, so we experimented with knitted techniques, using a circular knit to eliminate hard seams."

Seams that had hitherto been structural were instead transposed onto outer-garments, gesturing provocatively at the shape of the body beneath: under-wiring decorated denim, the vertical stitching of corsetry became a decorative element, and vivid motifs from outer garments decorated underwear. In Quant's hands underwear became outerwear and outwear took on features of underwear.

Men's boxer shorts became colourful hot pants visible under minis, (paradoxically both drawing attention to their bold sexiness and assuring their modesty); grandfather's vests were the starting point for a range of sporty T-shirts, whilst children's socks were pulled over the knee to create her 'Kooky School Girl' look.

Central to Quant's fashion revolution was the shifting of the erogenous zone to concentrate on the legs. Tights were perhaps, the most significant aspect of underwear, elevated by Quant to the importance of an outer garment, and a crucial part of a vocabulary of separates.

"Tights... there was nothing available on the market and stocking manufacturers were not interested in producing small editions of tights with rapidly changing styles... so I had to go to theatrical manufacturers who were used to it... eventually a gentleman called Mr. Curry invested in the equipment, and started production for us. We developed tights that were printed, textured, appliquéd...."

Strong statements as blocks of colour, tights acted as backdrops to mini pinafores, as important as the skinny rib sweaters, and, owing to the altered proportions of the mini, more visible. Legs were further accentuated by the emphasis placed on them in the fashion press, and by their representation in the work of photographers like David Bailey and Donovan. These photographers, famously associated with Quant, manipulated the image of legs

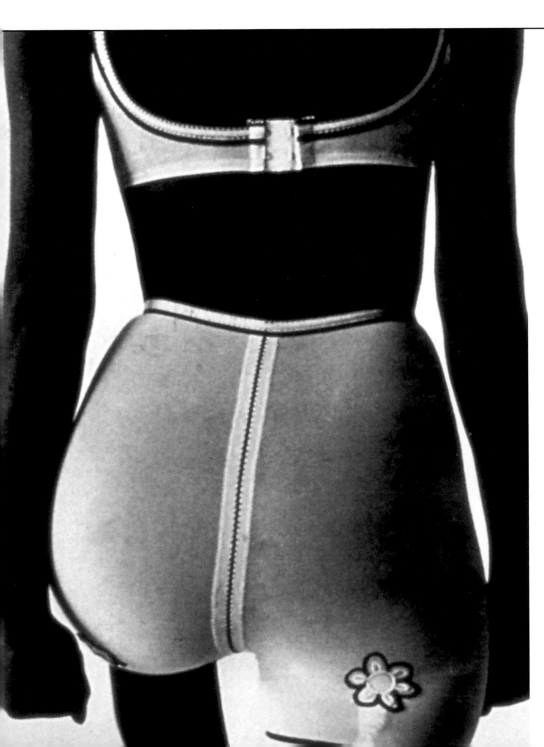

further by using a worm's eye view to elongate them.

The moment of expansion came when the huge American chain J.C. Penny, for whom she was a design consultant from 1962 to 1973, persuaded her to find a tights manufacturer in America. Suddenly Mary Quant was being sold worldwide.

Underwear played an important part of a careful layering that took Quant's clients from day to evening—"Fashion conscious careers girls" as Quant describes them, "went from where they had to be formal to a bar and then on to a club and needed something that could transform for each occasion, something that would become more transparent and sexy as the night went on... right through to going home, often with their partners...."

Mary Quant, with the help of her husband, was always involved in the whole process of fashion and its moods, from design, packaging, window display to the catchy naming of products, inventing the sort of evocative puns we continue to

'Underwear',
Mary Quant design,
1965

associate with magazine titles, creating
a blueprint for modern merchandising
practices. The simple, instantly recognisable
daisy logo now stands for an international
empire.

As we are viewing the much awaited
Autumn/Winter 2001 collections, invested
with Stanley Kubrick's fantasy, fragments
of Quant's language are self-consciously
quoted, others have been assimilated or
absorbed to such a degree they are no
longer so conspicuous. Sitting at her desk,
the surface of which is covered with
drawings, "Next week is Premier Vision
in Paris, tweed as light as air..." she muses.

Mary Quant designs,
1963

knee high

the best of british brought to their knees

photographed by sandro sodano

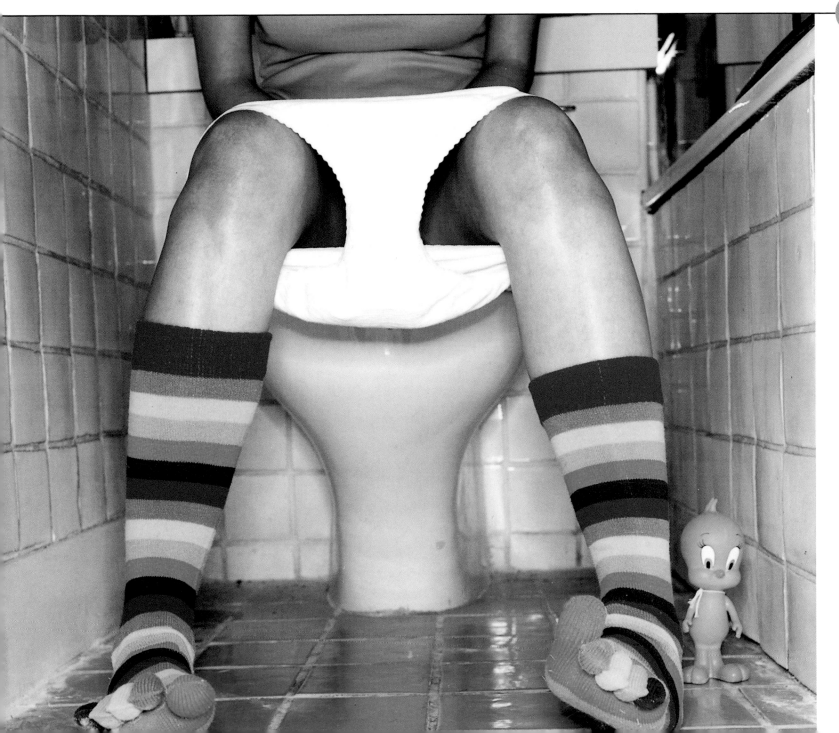

material world

James Pretlove with Alice Cicolini

a subject better left to the privacy of the closet? And also an industry with closer association to the quality of Italy, the haute couture of France, the marketing of the USA and technology of Japan. Yet for a country where underwear is usually seen, but not spoken of, the level of developments in the underwear industry and the application of technology to them is surprisingly high.

The value of the British design perspective, as Allen Jones has said, is "as a source of invention." Twin that with our prudish but decadent humour, and a love of re-invention and the re-application of materials, and the reason for focusing on British bras becomes more pertinent.

Underwear has inspired a wealth of visual imagery in Britain and continues to be a subject regularly plundered by our creative folk, commercially and artistically. From Babs Windsor losing her bra in *Carry on Camping* to Rhys Ifans flashing in *Notting Hill*, displaying our bras and briefs is a full time occupation on the screen. The list of pivotal British film movements that centre on underwear is as long as your thermals. From John Cleese in *A Fish Called Wanda* prancing the room in his old-school 'Y's, countless moments of flaunting far less than that in *The Full Monty* to rummaging in

Sadie Frost's laundry bin in *Final Cut* (who wouldn't?), this bawdy theatricality has been loved and lauded since Shakespeare's days at the Rose.

Not all our film moments are quite as schoolboy humour, as Peter Greenaway's sophisticated exploration of food, sex and danger, *The Cook, The Thief* shows. Helen Mirren isn't one of the UK's most stylish actresses for nothing and whilst we may rarely see her in her smalls, we certainly catch more than a glimpse of her fatal attraction. Whilst Mona Lisa wasn't necessarily a pinnacle of chic, it certainly captured humour and edge, sexuality and danger, in all its uniquely British glory.

Whilst Kate Winslet's knickers in *Hideous Kinky* might have been grubby, at least she had style. And "Bond, James Bond", will always be remembered for removing his, and others' briefs often.

What was sexy in Sean Connery, and occasionally in Roger Moore, was the slight of hand in divesting their girls of what underwear they had. What is perfect about Brosnan's Bond is that he has grasped the root of it all—he may be sophisticated and always get his girl, but it is the hint of potential failure in his naive schoolboyish bluster that makes Bond so quintessentially British.

Underwear proliferates on our TV and advertising billboards. The Trevor Beattie 'Hello Boys' campaign was a starting point, but the continuous stream of pants writ large that has followed has everything to do with a very British obsession that goes beyond the breasts.

previous page Barbara
Windsor in the film 'Carry
on Camping', 1969

From Internet search companies (www.lycos.co.uk) to Pot Noodle–'everything else is pants'–and the recent mail-shot campaign from a London-based advertising agency–'is your agency pants?'–the use of undergarments as objects of humour is ubiquitous. Alongside knickers and bras are tights, and Trevor Beattie has followed up 'Hello Boys' with the world's largest billboard shot of perfect legs for Pretty Polly.

Newspapers and magazines follow suit. *The Sun*'s Page Three has been a national treasure since the early 70s. In the 90s the vehicle that launched countless D-list celebrities from Samantha Fox to Jo Guest was re-invented as *Loaded*, the boy's toys magazine pioneered by its first editor James Brown. *Loaded* girls and their poorer cousins on the pages of *FHM* and *Front* have been pouring off the shelf into our sweaty palms for a decade. Bordering on 'top shelf' material, these magazines claim to be funny but more frequently offend, although *Loaded* claims that its readership is split almost 50/50 men and women.

At the other extreme of style, *Dazed & Confused*'s fashion editor Katie Grand, *Frank*'s stylist Charlotte Stockdale and photographers Corinne Day and Juergen Teller have all ransacked the national underwear drawer for fashionable inspiration. Grubby, sexy, granny, chic, ruffles, frills, boning and beads. The images are a striking melange of saucy bravado and sophisticated dering-do. Day's seminal photo shoot for *Vogue* with Kate Moss in the early 90s distilled the tone of her generation–stark, sexy, and with just enough dirtiness to make Kate Moss a contemporary icon, crowned by an underwear shoot.

The moment that Moss encapsulated was British club culture writ large. Always a rich influence on British fashion and visual language, the rave generation was the latest in a rich history of the dance floor inspiring the catwalk. No coincidence that designers and brands from Jean-Paul Gaultier to Levis trawl London's clubs and streets.

From the Beatles' 60s androgyny to The Rolling Stones' leathers and the Sex Pistols' bondage, the body and ways of displaying it have dominated the dance floor. Leigh Bowery in the 80s revelled in carnival-like decoration, disguise and performance art, at his club Taboo and on the international stage with dancer Michael Clark. Clark's partner at the time, David Holah, was half of design duo BodyMap, whose peekaboo Lycra designs questioned the traditional acceptance of what bits of the body are sexy. Boy George, Duran Duran and

Spandau Ballet all played with the girls-will-be-boys-and-boys-will-be-girls look, enhancing their sexual teen appeal with buckets of make-up and mountains of hairspray. 90s rave saw sexy androgyny take centre stage again, in parallel with the re-appearance of glam-trash in the form of DJ Jon of the Pleased Wimmin'.

The influence of all these cultural layers is clearest in fashion design. Alexander McQueen's bumsters acknowledge Bowery, as his Lycra cut-out collection does BodyMap. But it is no less apparent in the work of Britain's industrial and product designers. After meeting on a production, actresses Mina Anwar (from the TV series *The Thin Blue Line*), and Dervla Kerwan (from *Ballykissangel*) formed Aware International, a company producing and selling safe-sex underwear with a pouch for condoms which is much more practical and comfortable than your average chastity belt. The range plays on a 'pants' gag, a super club, girls on the town, *Loaded* attitude. Anwar and Kerwan sell their products over the Internet using the tools of popular culture –"the web's future is not to just buy something over the net, but to think and buy." Anwar is keen to emphasise that the range isn't just about sex. "It's about

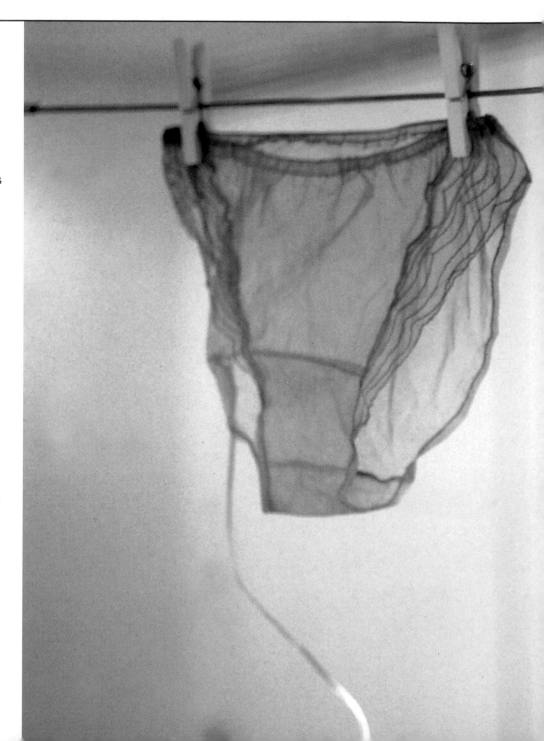

promoting the dangers of unprotected sex, not just unwanted pregnancy, but HIV and STDs by giving people the responsibility for themselves and their own safety."

Kursty Falconer's Techno bra translates high-tech protective electronics into a consumer-friendly product. The development came out of her Industrial Design Masters at the Royal College of Art. "What I really wanted to do was to combine my interest in materials and technology, and attack an area that I didn't really feel had been looked at before—a taboo subject such as violence or rape—but from a woman's point of view." Why fumble around in your handbag for a device, when you could be wearing protective underwear? "I was looking at wearable technology and learning from domestic violence workers and the police that there was a huge problem with the old-fashioned version of the personal alarm." Falconer developed a breastplate that could detect traumas as part of a bra. "Your heart-rate reacts in a totally different way to danger than to running, or even caffeine. I worked out a way to signify and interpret this. If you have been attacked it can position you, and send a pre-recorded text message wherever you want." Falconer was poached from the RCA by PDD, a company of product innovation consultants. The first product based on her research will be a sports bra. "It will monitor your heart rate, and talks to a receiver in a wrist watch or in the gym—a step further towards its realisation as an alarm."

PDD are also working with industrial designers, Seymour Powell, on a collaboration with British underwear manufacturers, Charnos. The Bioform takes the materials of the Frisbee and re-works them in a product that may yet revolutionise the underwear industry. They have reappraised bra engineering to create a comfortable, machine-washable and, above all, strangely beautiful solution to the increasingly large British bust.

Product designers Inflate have also been approached to re-work the bra, this time using inflatables to cosset and protect these precious attributes. Nick Crosbie, Inflate's design director, is looking at ways of creating a Libran balance that could see women, like Janus, with breasts pointing out in both directions. Far more interesting, at least to Crosbie, is his range of dip-moulded underwear. Inspired by Ursula Andress in *Dr. No*, the bra and briefs draw on trash-glam sentiments, but with a very Angus Deayton touch—the briefs contain a pocket, flush to the body, that holds your credit card. These briefs could literally take you round the world in your underwear.

The ultimate hope for the application of design and of new technologies to underwear in the UK lies with the country's colleges. Another graduate student at the Royal College of Art, Kim Si-Man, has designed underwear for the homeless that can be changed without taking off the outer clothing. De Montfort University in Leicester is the only college in the world with a course specifically designed for studies in the construction of underwear and other next-to-the-body clothing—the Contour Fashion degree. Heading it up is Janice Mee. "The course is unique worldwide. It started as a Corsetry Course in 1947 with five students and two lecturers. Now our graduates work for all the main players—Warners, Gossard, Berlei—three of them are at Victoria's Secret in the States."

The most exciting development for De Montfort now is that the Contour Fashion course, in conjunction with the Electrical Engineering Department, has been responsible for the C-Bra. Combining Dr. Wei Wang's development of electronic sensors within a bra from Mee's department, the C-Bra should be able to detect breast cancers, earlier and more easily than conventional mammography. GPs will also be able to link the bra up to a PC, through which a connection could be made with a consultant at a local hospital.

Subverting these kind of developments in underwear is artist-cum-craftsperson Hester Welsh. She came up with Smalls, a range of comedy underwear. "All the different pants are based on some sort of fact or news article—that's why they've got different names—and they're all recycled." The range runs to more than fifteen pairs of pants—from *Richard* virgin Y-fronts through *Eve* chastity pants to *Edna* piles pantees—and is continually expanding. The *Bored Housewife* pack is much awaited. All of Welsh's *Smalls* come with useful details—a furry strip inside the 'Richard' trainspotters Y-fronts "to keep out platform draughts", the chat-up lines printed on the waistband of the *Colin* Y-fronts "so first-daters can sneek-a-peek at them if needed." Welsh summarises perfectly the enduring and comic design appeal of underwear: "Basically, everyone's got hang ups about this or that but because everyone's also quite nosey, underwear is the perfect arena. It is such a private thing but also so telling."

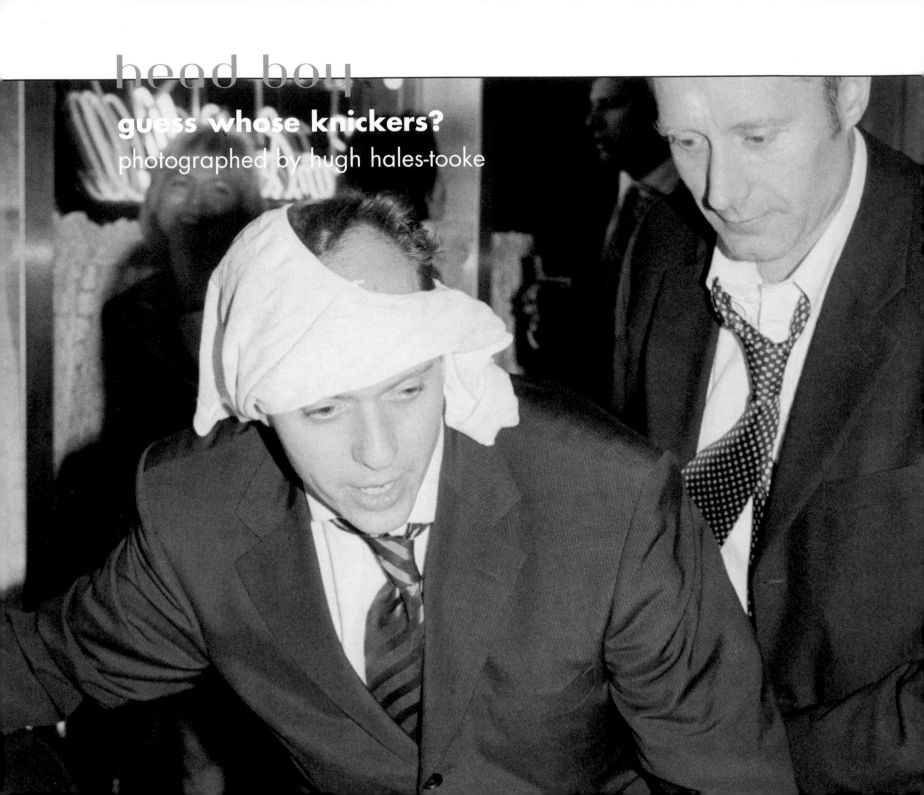

head boy

guess whose knickers?

photographed by hugh hales-tooke

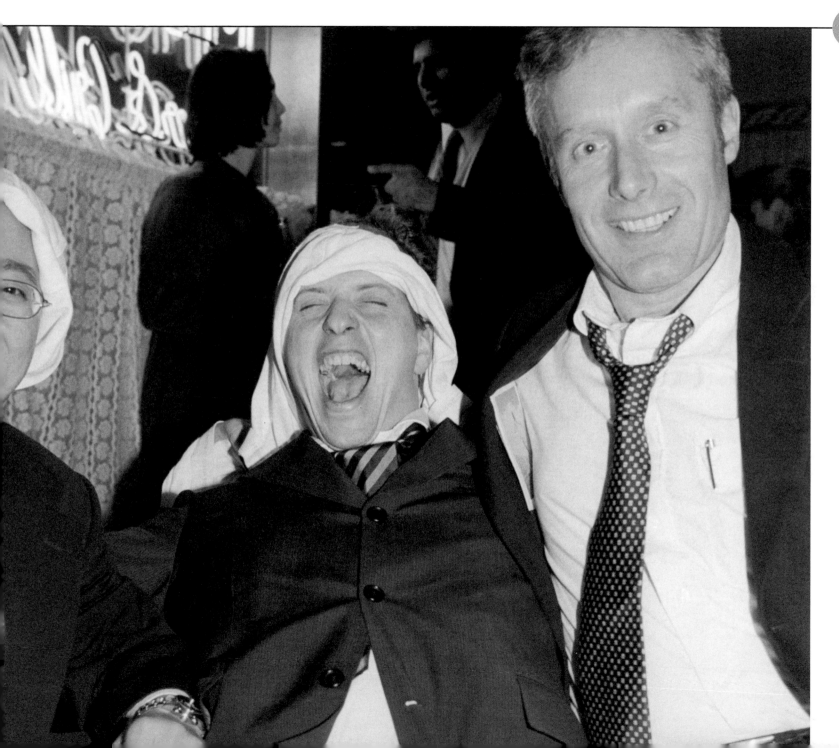

uber underwear

alice cicolini on allen jones

"In a world ordered by sexual imbalance, pleasure in looking has been split between active/male and passive/female. The determining male gaze projects its fantasy onto the female figure, which is stylised accordingly—coded for strong visual and erotic impact."

It's no coincidence that Pop artist Allen Jones should live in the heart of Clerkenwell, combining as it does London's artistic aristocracy *du jour* with the earthliness of Smithfield's blunt and bloody meat market.

His apartment is not an exhibition space for a lifetime of work; Lichtenstein prints sit at ease with Habitat cups, Jones own infamous *Hatstand* rests comfortably on a Persian rug. The delicate balance of old and new, pop-culture and High Art, scholarly calm and the physicality of urban life outside is a perfect analogy for Jones work.

Allen Jones has had an enormous influence on a generation of British designers, primarily those concerned with the body and the erotic. Designers from Whitaker Malem and Stella McCartney to Agent Provocateur have credited him as an inspiration. Jones' work, whilst using some of the language of fashion, was predominantly an exploration of new methods of representing the figure in art, and a desire to use new technology and fabrics as part of that process. He was also a great proponent of the sense of irreverence, mischief and sensuality which run throughout British art and design. All of which combine to explain his celebrated status at the turn of the century.

Allen Jones began his career at Hornsey School of Art in 1955. In 1959, a short period passed at the Royal College of Art in the company of David Hockney and R.B. Kitaj before Jones was unceremoniously thrown out after a year. He went on to complete post-graduate teacher training at Hornsey in 1961. By 1969, Jones had returned from an extended sojourn in America, and had begun the infamous furniture series of sculptures that were to throw him in direct conflict with the canons of feminist criticism.

Hatstand, Chair and *Table* (all 1969) were the primary cause of Jones' clash with the movement. Clay-modelled, fibreglass sculptures of women, they are dressed in the formal regalia of the S&M bordello; knee-high laced boots with leather hotpants and the regulation slick of red lipstick. Each sculpture is an exaggerated representation of Woman, and elicited extensive and sustained revulsion amongst the hardcore of militant feminists at Jones'

previous page 'Black
Breastplate', Allen Jones
1973
right Allen Jones with
'Hatstand', c.1995

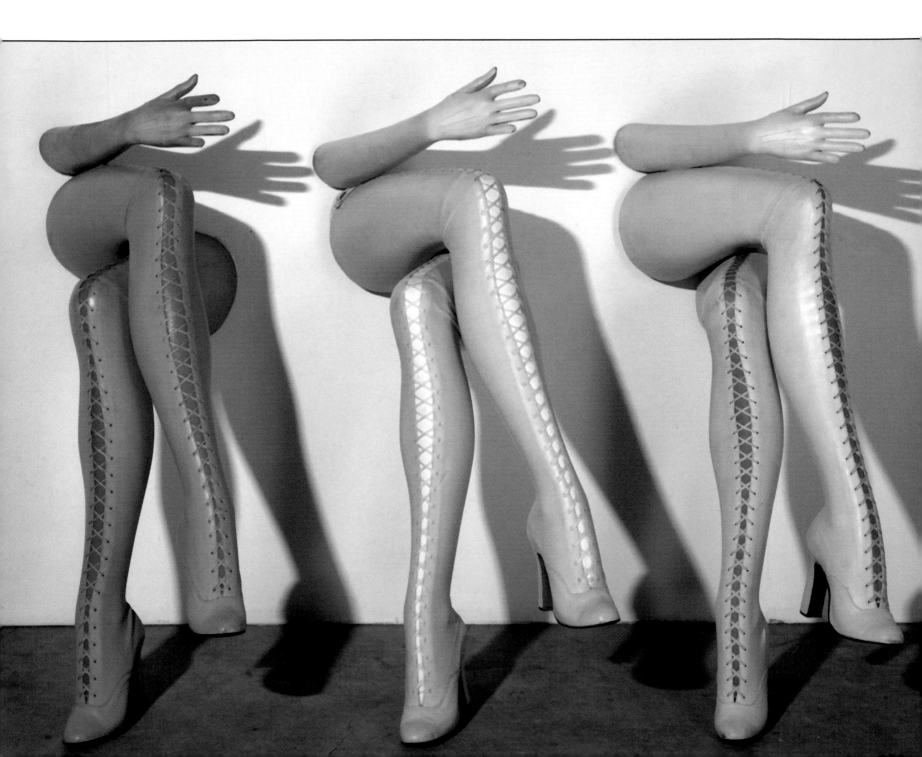

*'Secretary', Allen Jones
1972*

perceived exploitation of the female form.

For Jones, the sculptures played on a prescribed response to 'high art' forcing the viewer to contradict their natural motor response to everyday furniture. At the launch event in New York, Jones saw a woman about to place her empty wine glass on *Table*. "By chance our eyes met through the fog, because, of course, I was watching to see how people would react. She stopped herself in mid-movement and gestured is it alright? which to me was a sign that the work had been a success. It was up to her, her decision."

Jones still states that he's surprised that people were so shocked at the time. Surely this is disingenuous? It would be naive to suggest that the sculptures could not be interpreted in a more provocative light. Stripped of all the artist's intentions, and taken out of the context of the time in which they were made, the sculptures are ultimately women in compromising and subservient positions. Yet, as Jones says, "no matter what you might conclude from a semiotic analysis of the imagery, to discount the conscious agenda, or reason for the thing being done in the first place, is bad news." Jones continues to assert that the sculptures, and indeed paintings and illustrations of

the time, were "trying to offend the canons of art, not trying to offend people" by placing a certain widespread type of figurative art inside a gallery context.

Allen Jones claims his figures are no more provocative or lascivious than the naked and semi-naked figures that adorn the wall of the National Gallery were in their day. As he says, "they were painted as very private entities so to go into the National Gallery and look at paintings that were essentially some kind of horny turn-on is to automatically take them out of context."

Jones gleaned inspiration from the pages of catalogues like Frederick's of Hollywood that played on their ability, through illustration (rather than photography), to exaggerate the female form. Purveyors of a common and popular type of erotica, Frederick's of Hollywood was, and continues to be, at the forefront of imagery that sells a view of an outward, natural female sensuality (once selling 'Back to Nature' bottomless knickers). Jones states that he chose bordello gear for its exoticism, the commonly-held belief that these garments were separate from the everyday. The underwear defines the sculptures as completely as their positioning by dislocating the viewer.

One of Jones' primary goals was accentuating the figure, and the new materials of the time were the perfect tool.

"The end of the 60s and early 70s was a moment of fantastic development in the clothing industry. Fashion designers began to appropriate materials primarily developed for the sports industry, in which the body could be displayed yet covered."

By focusing on the body Jones was, he believed, highlighting the cultural focus on the body in a way that was in keeping with feminist theory, rather than in conflict with it. The figures were intended as empowering rather than derogatory, in–that they should have provoked debate concerning traditionally held beliefs rather than the commonly misinterpreted intentions of the artist.

Jones influence on the work of Agent Provocateur is most strongly identified in their use of colour, materials and the trappings of the exotic. Their distinctive combination of vibrant colour, tactile satins and silks, delicate ribbons and dominatrix chains and leather bondage has enticed women all over the world to highlight their bodies. Agent Provocateur's Serena Rees and Joe Corré have both cited Jones as an inspiration to the tone and feel of their brand.

"An important aspect of these images... is that you identify as much with the artist as with the work... Between you, the picture and its unseen creator exists a kind of affinity, as if you understand each other... it's up to you to explore the ideas they offer."

Whilst alluding to Jones' *Hatstand* and *Secretary* sculptures (1972), Rees and Corré make particular reference to Jones' *ShoeBox* series–his search for the iconic shoe. "The high-heeled black shoe became an inevitable choice. From Freud to Frederick's it is the archetypal shoe." Whilst acknowledging that the shoe is not strictly lingerie, Rees and Corré state: "...no erotic image of a beautifully undressed woman is complete without a heel of at least five inches. They are fuck-me-*if*-you-can-catch-me shoes, giving pleasure through the knowledge of the effect they can have on you, the powerless voyeur."

Designers Whitaker Malem, specialists in radical leather corsetry, declare a massive debt to Allen Jones. They are currently

working with Jones on an artist's proof set of the furniture series, creating garments that are as true to the originals as they are in keeping with the Whitaker Malem style. It is Jones' exploration of performance and display through dress that has most inspired their work. The leather corsets, for which they are best known, question sexuality, taking an erotically charged garment and creating almost identical versions for men and women. Whilst not shying away from the difference in body shape, the corsets create an identical, yet still sexual, image for both sexes. They believe that Jones sculptures intended to question drag in dress, the daily parody in which we all consciously or otherwise engage.

Jones worked fairly regularly designing costume for film and theatre performances, a natural extension of his art. Theatrical costume exploits exaggerated dress to create strong visual images, engaging in disguise and drag. The most significant piece of work using the language of underwear was Ken Tynan's theatrical review *Oh Calcutta!* Tynan's review was a collaborative work, including writing from Roman Polanski to John Lennon. Tynan, at the time, was fascinated with how historically recent the introduction of female knickers was into everyday wear. A piece written for *Playboy* sparked his interest in developing the germ of an idea into a full-blown theatrical exploration. In a book of letters, Tynan writes "A journalist in California asked me whether there was any difference between British and American sexual habits. I replied in what I hoped was a flippant tone, that it was well known that the English were far more decadent and perverse."

This was a statement he set out to illustrate more by (literally) uncovering great British icons from Queen Victoria to Jane Austen in *Oh Calcutta!*. Both vocal proponents of the virtues of modesty, Victoria and Austen almost certainly wore no knickers, and Tynan found the inherent, relatively contemporary contradiction hilarious, and typical of a Britishness that lauded exterior modesty whilst practising, he believed, the exact opposite behind closed doors.

Jones' designs for Tynan's contribution to the review responded to the tone of uncovering, of stripping away, by focusing attention on the actors lack of underwear.

"Tynans thesis was that tights, which were then the latest thing, were against sex because they made a person inaccessible. It seemed to me that, as nudity was not common on the

right and previous page
Scarlett O'Hara costume,
'Oh! Calcutta', Allen Jones
1970

'Chair', Allen Jones 1969

stage, if one could design a costume that actually covered the figure and left the pubic hair uncovered it would be a visual challenge to the audience, but maintain the performer's anonymity."

By keeping the costumes uniform, it helped to objectify the visual experience. So Scarlett O'Hara was dressed in bloomers attached to the knee, and the hoop skirt was covered only at the front; Jane Austen had a skirt as zimmer frame – step away from the frame and the author's true state of undress was revealed. Jones had found a flavour of latter-day theatrical bawdiness to re-invest the somewhat puritanical stage of the late 60s and 70s with shock value.

It's much harder to shock these days. Where times have changed for Rees and Corré is the lack of shock factor in their work. The enormous commercial success of the luxury, high-end sexual fashion that they offer bears testament to that. As Jones says, "it's a strange irony that something like Frederick's of Hollywood, which I discovered and collected 20 or 30 years ago and thought had some aesthetic merit, should have become validated."

Even more ironic that an artist inspired by commercial art has become an inspiration for retail in the future. "A lot of things, when I was starting out, that were elicit, not public or beyond the norm of public taste, had a strength that now one sees as being simply another decorative fashion device." In exposing the public to these elicit images Jones has created the cultural space for companies like Agent Provocateur to exist. And without the concurrent, dirty undertone associated with a 'real' sex shop like Ann Summers. "I do see myself, with detached irony, as embedded in that process."

"In a way," Jones suggests, "in a revolutionary situation you have to be extreme, so the burning bra period could be seen as necessary to galvanise the public awareness concerning female representation. But of course, that's exactly what the artist is doing all the time."

size matters

photographed by martin parr

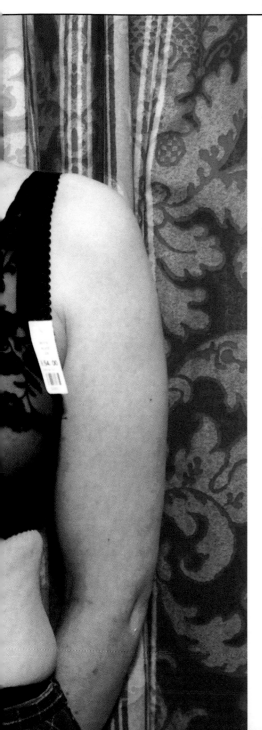

been fitted for a bra. Most mass-produced bras only accomodate the shape and size of about 10% of women. In a discrete Knightsbridge boutique, and in an overflowing shop in East London, there are two women who can size you up at twenty paces without so much as a measuring tape. Mrs. Kenton, of Rigby & Peller, holds the Royal Warrant for corsetry and is an internationally regarded expert on fit and form. Carol of Stepney has fitted some of the most challenging bosoms in Britain, from mastectomy patients to period actresses, Page Three girls to brides.

everything erotic

an interview with joseph corré & serena rees

karen kay

start? Did you set out to have a lingerie
brand called Agent Provocateur...

Joseph Corré We thought of the name
Agent Provocateur a long time before we
actually did anything with it. We originally
had a much bigger idea, which was going
to be a small department store for
everything to do with the erotic. We tried
for a couple of years to raise the finance
and to find the location and in the end we
decided we couldn't wait anymore. That was
October and we were open by December.
The name Agent Provocateur fitted perfectly
with what we were doing. It represents a
small spark that has a large effect–the guy
that throws the first stone in a volatile
situation and gets the crowd going.

Serena Rees I don't think we set out
to create a brand. Originally we started
buying in from other suppliers, but we found
there wasn't anything out there exciting and
interesting enough, so we started designing
and then producing ourselves.

J I think you can certainly say that as a
consequence of what we've done in the last
five years, lingerie and underwear have

been placed fairly and squarely on the fashion map. It's now something that both high street and couture ends of fashion design take seriously. We've said, "This is something that is absolutely sexy and the ramifications of that within your own daily life are really interesting." It's nothing to be ashamed of and we just put it in front of people's noses.

S Before, if you wanted something really sexy and naughty, you'd have to go and buy something cheap and tacky from a sex shop. If you wanted something that was very good quality—beautiful fabrics and properly fitted—you might have to go to a specialist who would create something made-to-measure. Then if you wanted something fashionable... well, that was almost impossible to find and it probably didn't fit very well. You'd be running around all over Europe trying to find this thing, whereas we brought it all together and we're real specialists in what we do.

J We've been constantly labelled as people who've managed to find this gap in the market and I hate that sort of terminology. We certainly never think about what trends are and what colour is 'this season.' What we did was just look honestly at the product

and ask "what does this represent to us and what should it represent?" We came up with the same things again and again: glamour, a sense of luxury, a sense of comfort, fit, intimacy, of passion, of service, of people who know what they're talking about. We took all of those elements and created the shop around what we were selling.

K Do you think Agent Provocateur could have happened anywhere else?

J We're a nation of shopkeepers. It's relatively easy to open a shop. If you were a young guy in Italy and wanted to do the same thing, it's virtually impossible without having your whole family put down their life savings and mortgage their house to do it. The infrastructure is here to exploit your own ideas and I think that's something that's very good about the UK. But I think you get let down at the other end, producing things and investing in skills.

S We always thought to ourselves that there was a place somewhere—it might have been in Paris or maybe New York... wherever—but a place like our store, where you could go and buy a present for someone, or for yourself. But it never really existed. I think it

previous page Photograph for the Agent Provocateur mail order catalogue, 1999 right Interior of Agent Provocateur's original shop in Broadwick Street, Soho

was important that it started here. We opened in Soho because of the history of the sex industry and it's a very busy part of town, people drink and eat there, work there, live there. Also, being on one of the main shopping streets in London is incredibly expensive, I mean Sloane Street or Bond Street... it's impossible.

J Our idea was not about being exclusive. It was about saying this really is for everybody, whether you want to spend £5 or £5000. It doesn't really matter, you'll be treated in the same way. I certainly like the fact that you have a schoolgirl buying something standing next to pop star in the same queue, feeling relaxed and looked after and comfortable in that environment.

K Because you have such a diverse range of customers, how do you go about designing?

S We don't watch market trends and things like that. I don't think we put anything in the stores that we don't like or that I wouldn't wear myself or maybe that Joe wouldn't like to see me wearing. The nice thing is, we have a huge variety. We might take a particular style and colour that is not immediately suitable to, say, a 70 year old woman but she might think it's suitable for her and she wants to wear it. We offer an enormous range of sizes so that anybody that does want to wear that style can. Each person needs a particular shape of bra so we try and provide a good choice which helps all different ages, styles and tastes. We have some things that are a bit more sexy than others, we have some things that people would want to wear everyday and some that you'd only want to wear for evening. We do bedroom wear... we do corsetry.... We can fulfil everyone's different fantasies and it seems to work, doesn't it?

K Do you think it helps that you're lovers as well as business partners?

J Absolutely. I think what's really good about our situation and our partnership is that we have both the male and female perspective on underwear. Sometimes one of us is adamant about a particular style or something that the other, perhaps, doesn't like and we'll say "Well it's good that we disagree, let's do it anyway." We're very strong independently of each other, but we're sort of even stronger when we're together, which is great.

K How do you work together? is there pillow talk involved?

J I think a lot of inspiration comes from fabrics and colours. When we initially started we were heavily influenced by 1950s underwear. Not because we were retro mad, but because the shapes and the construction of these garments was just so much more interesting. They were very inspiring because of the fantasies built into them. There was a sense of detail and consideration in them that you couldn't find anywhere else. In the high street it's about putting as little into the garment as they can in order to sell it at the price that's cheaper than next door, but then they add some gimmick to make you want it. That was completely opposite to what we were looking at in those vintage garments; they were about the inside being as nice as the outside, about really experimenting with different types of fabrics next to each other to achieve the right fit and shape. It was about a certain freeness of design and use of colour.

S It's much more difficult than when you're designing dresses because some of the best fabrics you can't wash. And obviously people have to able to wash their underwear and it's a shame really because there are some incredible fabrics.

J Yeah... can you imagine sending your knickers to the dry cleaners?

S We just think that's a bit beyond reality...

K Do you think it's important to have a sense of humour in underwear?

S Absolutely. Despite the fact that we're serious in the way that we provide a service in our stores, there is still room for a sense of humour and Britons do have that kind of "nudge-nudge-wink-wink-ha-ha-going-into-a-lingerie-shop" approach still. I think the fact that people want to have fun, dress up and enjoy it, comes over in some of our designs, don't you ?

J Oh absolutely, I was just thinking about that daisy thing... sometimes you get things and they just make you howl with laughter.

S You have to... I'll explain it to you. It was a little very itsy bitsy tiny bikini and basically all it was was a bit of elastic that went around the waist and a daisy on both

nipples and then one on the front of the bikini... that was it. It was very funny and maybe I might not have worn it myself on the beach but I thought it was great on somebody else and they sold out like that, you know, just ran out of the door.

K Serena, what do you think is sexy?

S Sexy can mean lots of different things. There's girlie sexy, then there's womanly sexy, there's dominatrix sexy, there's saucy sexy. But things that make me personally feel sexy are things that make me feel good about myself. That's what we aim to do for other people and it's different for everybody and it's different every day.

K Do you think a certain piece of underwear can make a woman sexy?

S Yes, for example, the way something can make you stand or hold yourself, immediately changes you. A corset makes a woman sit up properly, feel proud and tall, pulls her in in all the right places, makes her really feminine. Maybe she didn't feel sexy before and there you are: she's sexy. I think most women are sexy, they've just gotta find it. Some people haven't found it.

K What do you think is sexy, Joe, from a male perspective?

J I would say that apart from the sensation of touch, talking purely visual, it's about the way that underwear frames and draws attention to certain parts of the female anatomy. That's why suspenders are sexy, because they draw both from the back and the front, they frame to me the most obvious sexy part of a woman's body. It's why certain bras are sexy because they enhance and make something extraordinary; they take the ordinary and make it exotic. That's probably something that's fairly primitive in all of us, it's about exoticising things. That's why birds of paradise do a little dance and put all their feathers up, it's why Brazilian carnival queens dance the way they do and put head dresses on, it's about taking something ordinary and making it extraordinary, or something human and making it superhuman.

K How do you think other countries perceive what you're doing?

S I think in every city there's women who want to feel the way women do in this country. They all come to our store here and

buy very, very differently and all have a different idea about what's sexy. The French and the Germans and the Italians... they're all quite different, the things they choose. Germans... I think Germans go for quite strict things... they really go for 'hard sexy'... the French go for pretty sexy and sophisticated sexy. I shouldn't really generalise but those are the trends that I've noticed... Americans, they go for everything and... the Japanese are a bit shy on see-through fabrics.

K What about the British ?

S British? Oh, they like everything. They'll have a real assortment. They seem to buy most things... yeah, they buy all of it, they're not so particular really, do you find that.

K Can you tell me a bit about the diversity of the customers? You said earlier that you had school girls next to pop stars?

J We do just have everybody.

S Everybody... taxi drivers to city gents to politicians, housewives to 'working ladies'. What's nice is getting somebody who really has saved up and it's really special for them to come and get something and they feel so thrilled. Everything gets gift-wrapped and they get this beautiful pink box with a ribbon around it and they rush out of the door and they feel great and they can't wait to get home, open their box and get their underwear on. It is a wonderful feeling watching people enjoy it like that. When we first opened I remember people were just popping their head through the door and saying "this is incredible, this is fantastic, where have you been all my life?", and that was really rewarding. The great thing about underwear is that it appeals to everybody; every age, whatever they do for a living, wherever they live, however much money they earn, everybody's interested in lingerie.

K Is there a difference between the two stores? Do Pont Street and Broadwick Street have different customers?

S In Knightsbridge there's this sort of Belgravia woman who shops. Less people shop in our Knightsbridge store, but they spend more money. In Soho you get a lot more people. Even though it's tiny, it's like the flagship store and people like to go there. All the customers have a preferred shop. It would have been really easy to take the idea from Soho to Knightsbridge and do the same theme, but the colour in Broadwick Street—it's Empire Red, it's really Soho, it's a passionate colour, quite heavy—was maybe too much for Knightsbridge. We wanted to lighten it up, make it more elegant perhaps. Whereas Soho's more... what is Soho?

J More rough and ready...

S And more sensuous. It's really a seductive boudoir and Knightsbridge is an elegant boudoir. We're working with the theme of chinoiserie in both stores, just taken in slightly different directions.

K You put pink pads around lamp posts outside the shop once... tell me about that?

S In Broadwick street, right opposite our window, is a lamp post... The amount of times that people have been so busy looking into the window, walking along... looking, looking, looking and then... bang! So we put up a nice pink padding on it which, of course, Westminster Council took down immediately. Our windows are quite exciting. We've had some quite good ones and Joe really enjoys it because it's a forum to say whatever he wants...

J It's something that we enjoy playing with and we're able to put in whatever we want. On certain occasions we've had the police come and tell us to remove it, other times people spit on the window...

S The neighbours complain...

J Whatever... but it certainly does the job about making people think twice about things. I remember that Brent Spar thing when Shell Oil were going to dump in the sea and we did an anti-Shell window. We took out all the newspaper cuttings and enlarged them and said what everybody else in Germany was doing, bombing Shell petrol stations. In England, where it was happening, nobody was doing very much at all. Even the guy in the Shell garage didn't know what was going on.

S I think it's great because although this is a business and it's doing well, we really enjoy it... we really have fun with it.

J We did a demonstration outside London Fashion Week, which was hilarious. We ran a Miss World-type competition to find Miss Agent Provocateur and we got down to 12 finalists and they all paraded with banners

Stills from a video interview with Serena Rees and Joe Corré, 2000

saying "put the passion back in fashion" and "more S&M less M&S" and "come and see our knickers" and "lust" in all this wonderful underwear. They stopped all the traffic, the police turned up and everything... The finalists jumped on the police and smothered them with kisses.

S We'd rather do things like that than advertise. We'd rather throw a great party or do something that's fun, not just for us but for other people too. It's a lot more rewarding, a lot more people enjoy it and it's cheaper than taking a page in magazine. It works... works really well.

K What are your future plans for Agent Provocateur?

S We've always maintained that Agent Provocateur can be anything we want it to be. We can have a restaurant, a bar, a hotel... whatever. We're planning to open more stores in major cities worldwide, but we're going to be quite careful about that, we don't want to be everywhere. We only want to have our own stores. I think the USA is next, and then after that we can decide the rest..

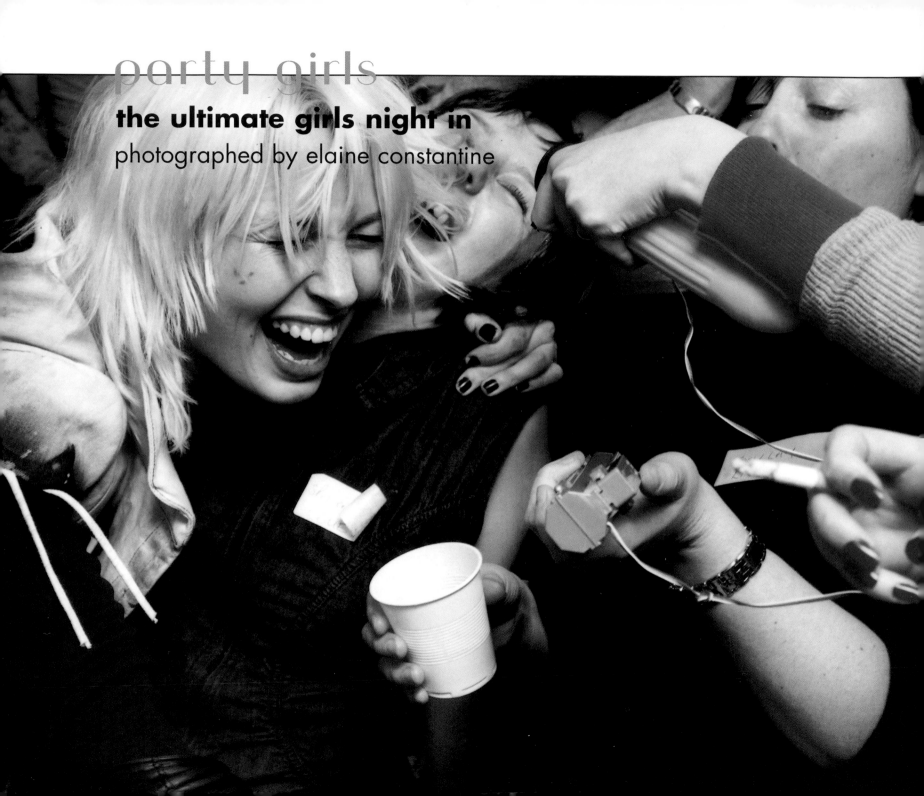

party girls

the ultimate girls night in
photographed by elaine constantine

David Gold and his father 'Goddy' opened Rosie's Bookshop on London's Charing Cross Road. The first Gold family venture, Rosie's was the seed of a multi-million pound business we now know as Ann Summers. The Ann Summers sex shop and mail order chain was originally a small subsidiary of the main business, publishing, which had earnt 'Goddy' and his family a reputation as London's very own Porn Barons.

It wasn't until 1981 that Ann Summers found its niche with David's daughter, Jacqueline Gold, at the helm. At a party with friends, Gold found herself passing around sex aids and lashings of latex over a glass of white wine. Whilst everyone loved the sexy lingerie, Gold discovered that most would never enter an Ann Summers store to buy it. Why not arrange parties? Following the lucrative example of Tupperware and Avon cosmetics, and the advice of her friends, Gold launched the Ann Summers Party Plan. Now with a party hotline, a party website, over 7,500 Party Organisers and five overseas shops in the pipeline, Ann Summers is the most successful purveyor of erotica in the UK.

dual controls   Diana Dors © Pictorial Press (www.pictorialpress.co.uk),
'Hello Boys' © TBWA, Leigh Bowery by Fiona Freund
vested interest   © Jeremy Murch *styling* Sarah Richardson
if the nude is rude...   Photographer unknown © Janet Reger
© Angela Carter 1978. Reproduced by permission of the Estate of Angela Carter
c/o Rogers, Coleridge & White Ltd., 20 Powis Mews, London W11 1JN.
luxe lingerie   Photographer unknown © Janet Reger
show us your bra   © Sandro Sodano
sea change   © Ben Ingham
a ceremony in itself   © Roberto Tecchio, courtesy Judith Clark Costume
film foundations   All images by Matthew Andrews
high performance   © Platon courtesy Billy's Topless Bar, a true New York institution
q-form   © Mary Quant
knee high   © Sandro Sodano, *model* Lilina Dominguez @ Premier, *styling* Sophia Neophitou
material world   Barbara Windsor © Pictorial Press (www.pictorialpress.co.uk),
Placebo underwear by Ed Reeve
head boy   © Hugh Hales-Tooke
uber-underwear   'Black breastplate' © Brian Duffy, Allen Jones © Thomas Hoepker, Magnum,
Scarlett O'Hara costume, for Kenneth Tynan's 'History of Knickers' sketch,
'Oh! Calcutta' © Allen Jones,   'Secretary' © Allen Jones,   'Chair' © Tate Gallery
size matters   © Martin Parr
everything erotic   Agent Provocateur mail order catalogue by Tim Brett-Day, Agent
Provocateur interiors by Julian Anderson, Agent Provocateur video by Karen Kay and
Simon Oliver © The British Council
party girls   © Elaine Constantine

colophon

© 2000 Black Dog Publishing Limited, The British Council and the authors

conceived and edited Emily Campbell and Alice Cicolini
editorial consultant Judith Clark
production Izzy King and Duncan McCorquodale
art direction and design Alan Aboud and Sara Hodge at Aboud•Sodano

Printed in the European Union.
Colour Origination Colourwise ltd.

ISBN 1 901033 27 9

British Library cataloguing-in-publication data. A catalogue record for this book is
available from The British Library.

Black Dog Publishing Limited PO Box 3082 London NW1 UK
T 44 (020)7 692 2697 F 44 (020)7 692 2698 e-mail info@bdp.demon.co.uk

The British Council is the United Kingdom's international organisation for educational and cultural relations. Its purpose is to enhance the reputation of the United Kingdom in the world as a valued partner.

The British Council promotes British design through our network in 110 countries in a programme of touring exhibitions, publications, overseas workshops and seminars and visit programmes in the UK. We work in partnership with other organisations and individuals in the production and delivery of these resources, including designers, publishers, government agencies, private corporations, universities, museums, galleries and cultural institutions.

The British Council's design promotion programme represents the diversity and quality of design practice in Britain. It covers industrial design, graphic design, architecture and the built environment, interior design and furniture, fashion, new media and cross-disciplinary work. Our aim is to extend the influence of British designers overseas and to encourage the local development of design in other countries.

This book is published in conjunction with the British Council's international touring exhibition *inside out: underwear and style in the UK*.

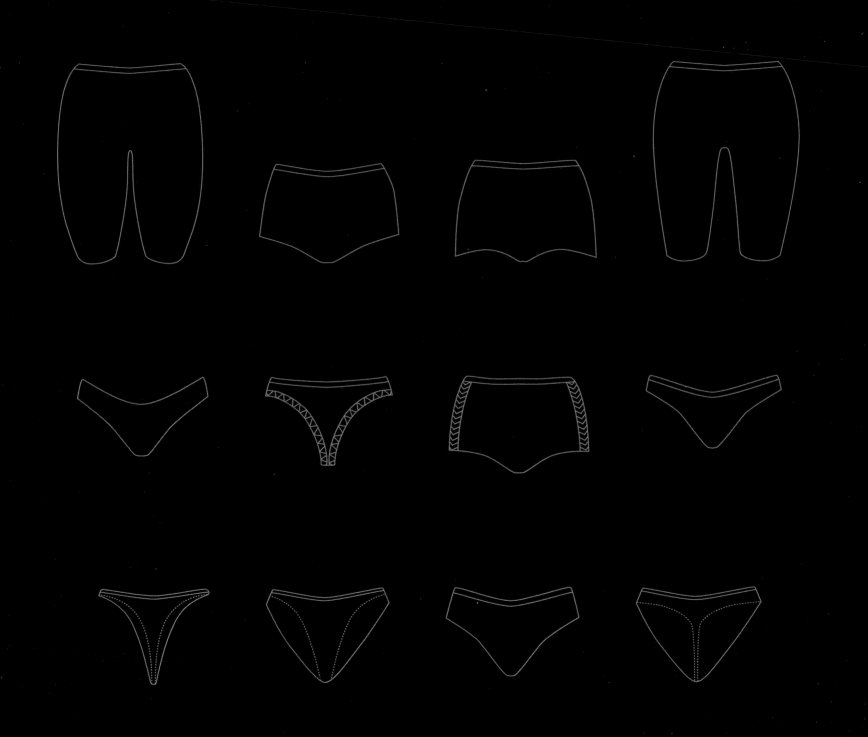